AF738348

Palgrave Studies in Classical Liberalism

Series Editors
David F. Hardwick
Department of Pathology and Laboratory Medicine
The University of British Columbia
Vancouver, BC, Canada

Leslie Marsh
Department of Pathology and Laboratory Medicine
The University of British Columbia
Vancouver, BC, Canada

This series offers a forum to writers concerned that the central presuppositions of the liberal tradition have been severely corroded, neglected, or misappropriated by overly rationalistic and constructivist approaches.

The hardest-won achievement of the liberal tradition has been the wrestling of epistemic independence from overwhelming concentrations of power, monopolies and capricious zealotries. The very precondition of knowledge is the exploitation of the epistemic virtues accorded by society's situated and distributed manifold of spontaneous orders, the DNA of the modern civil condition.

With the confluence of interest in situated and distributed liberalism emanating from the Scottish tradition, Austrian and behavioral economics, non-Cartesian philosophy and moral psychology, the editors are soliciting proposals that speak to this multidisciplinary constituency. Sole or joint authorship submissions are welcome as are edited collections, broadly theoretical or topical in nature.

More information about this series at
http://www.palgrave.com/gp/series/15722

Christopher Adair-Toteff

Carl Schmitt on Law and Liberalism

palgrave
macmillan

Christopher Adair-Toteff
Traunstein, Bayern, Germany

ISSN 2662-6470 ISSN 2662-6489 (electronic)
Palgrave Studies in Classical Liberalism
ISBN 978-3-030-57117-7 ISBN 978-3-030-57118-4 (eBook)
https://doi.org/10.1007/978-3-030-57118-4

© The Editor(s) (if applicable) and The Author(s), under exclusive licence to Springer Nature Switzerland AG 2020
This work is subject to copyright. All rights are solely and exclusively licensed by the Publisher, whether the whole or part of the material is concerned, specifically the rights of translation, reprinting, reuse of illustrations, recitation, broadcasting, reproduction on microfilms or in any other physical way, and transmission or information storage and retrieval, electronic adaptation, computer software, or by similar or dissimilar methodology now known or hereafter developed.
The use of general descriptive names, registered names, trademarks, service marks, etc. in this publication does not imply, even in the absence of a specific statement, that such names are exempt from the relevant protective laws and regulations and therefore free for general use.
The publisher, the authors and the editors are safe to assume that the advice and information in this book are believed to be true and accurate at the date of publication. Neither the publisher nor the authors or the editors give a warranty, expressed or implied, with respect to the material contained herein or for any errors or omissions that may have been made. The publisher remains neutral with regard to jurisdictional claims in published maps and institutional affiliations.

Cover illustration: © Pattadis Walarput/Alamy Stock Photo

This Palgrave Macmillan imprint is published by the registered company Springer Nature Switzerland AG.
The registered company address is: Gewerbestrasse 11, 6330 Cham, Switzerland

Für Stephanie-wie immer

Preface

This study was prompted by a growing sense of concern stemming from the increasing number of illiberal regimes in the world. Those leaders have differing reasons for condemning liberal democracy, but they all share the repudiation of liberal democracy's philosophical foundations. It also grew out of the realization that one of liberal democracy's most famous critics was the German constitutional scholar Carl Schmitt. He was a relentless critic of liberalism because he was convinced that it failed to secure order and safety in the state. It failed because it was too pluralistic and too tolerant. In addition, its adherents believed in reason and law and the benefits of discussion. Schmitt countered that pluralism weakened the state and discussions were unhelpful when decisions were demanded. Furthermore, he was convinced that reason was overrated and that law was applicable primarily during normal circumstances. During the 1920s and early 1930s, Germany was not under normal circumstances but had experienced numerous states of emergencies. Of course, Schmitt's criticisms undermined the Weimar government and led to Hitler's rise. We are not yet in a similar situation as Germany was then; nonetheless, there are too many troubling parallels. Given this, I believe that it would be highly instructive to examine his criticisms and thereby be better able to defend law and liberalism.

Over the course of five years, I have learned much about Carl Schmitt's philosophy from the writings of many other Schmitt scholars.

These include Joseph W. Bendersky, David Dyzenhaus, Duncan Kelly, John P. McCormick, Reinhard Mehring, William E. Scheuerman, and Stanley L. Paulson. I have also benefitted from comments from my fellow editors at *Carl-Schmitt-Studien*. I would like to thank Leslie Marsh for the continuous support and the continuing opportunity to write for him. Finally, I want to thank my wife Stephanie, the other "Prof. Dr. Adair-Toteff," for both her encouragement and her criticism—"wie immer."

100 Jahre Todestag Max Weber

Traunstein, Germany
Juni 20, 2020

Christopher Adair-Toteff

Contents

1	**Carl Schmitt's Philosophy**	1
2	**From Normal Justice to Exceptional Law: 1912–1919**	9
3	**Law, Politics, and Sovereignty: 1919–1923**	25
4	**Chaos Versus Dictator: 1924–1926**	47
5	**Politics or Law: 1927–1928**	61
6	**Constitutional Issues: 1928–1931**	75
7	**Constitutional Chaos and Political Turmoil: 1930–1932**	91
8	**Schmitt and the Recovery of Law and Liberalism**	113
	Index	125

1

Carl Schmitt's Philosophy

Abstract This chapter is an introductory chapter in which the main theme of this book is simply stated. It places Schmitt and his writings in their historical and political contexts. It provides an overview of the chapters and offers a few remarks about the scope of this book and the values that guide it.

Keywords Philosophy • Liberalism • Nazism • Life • Law

The name Carl Schmitt draws mostly negative responses because of his association with and the defense of the Nazis during the years 1933–1936. But even his most bitter detractors recognize that he was one of Germany's most important thinkers and was a leading constitutional scholar of the times. He was not only a great thinker and scholar; he was also a literary master. His writings during the 1920s were widely read and commented upon, in large measure because he was such a penetrating critic of German liberalism and its belief in the rule of law. Schmitt also believed in law; yet, he was convinced that law was political like almost everything else. He was a critic of liberalism as well, but his objections were not founded

© The Author(s) 2020

C. Adair-Toteff, *Carl Schmitt on Law and Liberalism*, Palgrave Studies in Classical Liberalism, https://doi.org/10.1007/978-3-030-57118-4_1

so much on the notion of liberalism itself; rather, he was convinced that its belief in discussion and toleration was misguided and that it threatened the unity of the state. Under normal circumstances, this would be problematic, but during the Weimar period Germany was anything but normal. Hundreds of books have been written on Germany's history between 1919 and 1933 and undoubtedly hundreds of books will be written in the future. Here, the barest of outlines will be offered in order to place Carl Schmitt's writings from this period into context. But in order to understand Weimar, one must have some sense of what brought Weimar into being.

Prior to 1914 Germany had moved from a mostly agrarian state to a major industrial power. By 1914, France and Britain had become suspicious of its designs and the outbreak of the war in August 1914 seemed to confirm their fears. Although the war began favorably for Germany, by 1915 there were concerns that victory might not happen. Yet, the leaders assured the population that Germany would soon be victorious. As the war dragged on, Germany suffered mounting disasters—massive casualties, food shortages, and in the fall of 1918, considerable unrest. November saw Germany's defeat, revolution, and the Kaiser's abdication and subsequent flight. During the first half of 1919 there were major discussions regarding how Germany would be reconstructed and the task of drawing up a new constitution was delegated to Hugo Preuss. The result was the Weimar constitution ("Weimarer Reichsverfassung") which was adopted in August of that year. The period between then and 1933 moved from an early period of political and economic upheaval to a time of relative calm, to the final years of economic collapse and political chaos. Throughout this time, Carl Schmitt was among the leading legal theorists. But what distinguished him from many others was his constant critique of liberalism and its belief in the normalcy of law. He believed that its foundation was insufficient to meet the crises that he saw unfolding and those that he warned would be occurring within the near future.

In 1934 Carl Schmitt published a brief article entitled "Der Führer schütz das Recht" ("The Führer Protects the Law"). This article has been taken as an indication of Schmitt's most loyal allegiance to Adolf Hitler and as a real indication that Schmitt was the "crown jurist of the Third Reich." There is much in this article to support those claims: Schmitt argued that Hitler had been warning for years that Germany was in danger, both from external enemies and from internal traitors. As such, Schmitt contended that Hitler earned the right and the power to establish a new order, one that was not based upon empty legalisms but was founded on true justice. The Führer was the protector of the law and earned the right to be the highest judge. In Schmitt's view, the Führer could do no wrong (Schmitt 1988b: 199–203). For the next several years Schmitt vociferously defended the Nazi regime but in 1936 his support was questioned and he fell from grace.

For Schmitt's opponents, his life after 1936 was payback for being a Nazi defender. Not only had Schmitt been banished from the high ranks of the Nazis, but after the war he was imprisoned, first by the Russians and then detained twice by the Americans. When he was finally released in 1947, he went into exile in Germany. While some friends visited him and an increasing number of scholars trekked to his home, he rarely left his village of Plettenberg. For many of his critics, his life after 1936 until his death was not just "Schadenfreude" but was a fitting end to one of the most vocal propagandists for the Third Reich. However, that is beside the point here. Schmitt's claim that the Führer was the protector of the law was primarily a conclusion of his arguments throughout most of his life prior to 1935 and that was that Germany was being rendered helpless because of its misplaced belief in law and liberalism. Because Germans were trusting empty legalisms and engaging in fruitless discussions, the nation was not recognizing the need for emergency measures. What was needed was not talk of tolerance and equality but direct action against Germany's enemies. Schmitt believed that he was living through extraordinarily troubling times and he likened himself to someone else who also wrote of protection and obedience—Thomas Hobbes. Some scholars have regarded Hobbes as the "Apostle of Fear" and they may be right. But I suggest that Carl Schmitt is also entitled to that name because he, too, insisted on the necessity for public security and order. I will leave it up to Hobbes scholars to determine how closely Schmitt followed Hobbes' political philosophy. What I am attempting to do is to show how the threat to security and order motivated much of Schmitt's writings from 1912 until 1932. Schmitt was in error to believe that a strong leader was the only defense a nation had but he was correct in much of his criticism of law and we would be wise to learn from his complaints about liberalism.

In the "Vorwort" to his 1940 collection of articles and speeches entitled *Positionen und Begriffe. In Kampf mit Weimar-Genf-Versailles 1923–1939*, Carl Schmitt wrote that as Heraclitus had insisted one could never go through the same river twice, one could never give the same speech or write the same article twice.[1] His point was that as time passes and circumstances change, one cannot maintain the same exact position that one previously had. Instead, one must realistically adapt to the present situation. The point here is that Schmitt did change his mind during the period under consideration and he altered his approach as the change in circumstances warranted. Nonetheless, during most of this period Schmitt never wavered in holding to two of his core convictions: first, that Germany was under siege from within as much as without and, second, that the belief in law and liberalism was not only naïve, but was a clear and present danger to the nation. Some scholars have considered Carl Schmitt to be wrong politically, but nevertheless regarded him as one of Germany's leading jurists while many others have dismissed his legal writings and have rejected him for his politics. My contention is that during the period under consideration, he was one of the best constitutional scholars that Germany had and that he was one of the most trenchant critics of liberalism in Europe. As such, we have much to learn from him about the limits of law and liberalism. Because my account ends in 1932, I will not need to address his Nazi affiliation or his postwar marginalization. Equally important is the fact that, with the exception of a few comments in the conclusion, I have refrained from making value judgments about Schmitt's positions on law and liberalism. My purpose here is to understand Schmitt's criticisms, not to condemn him. Schmitt has had many detractors and few defenders, but the former often wished to vilify him while the latter sometimes tried to lionize him. I deliberately choose to avoid both sides; I have striven to understand him. In so doing, I have sought to adhere to Max Weber's distinction between facts and values, between scholarship and partisanship. Scholarship strives

[1] "Man kann, sagt Heraklit, nicht zweimal durch denselben Fluß gehen. So, kann man auch nicht zweimal dieselbe Rede halten oder denselben Aufsatz schreiben" (Schmitt 1988a: 5).

for objectivity but values are subjective. I will leave these issues regarding Carl Schmitt's values and beliefs to others to consider; my concern is with his constant complaint that law and liberalism cannot guarantee public security and order. In certain respects, Carl Schmitt can be regarded as a modern-day Thomas Hobbes and can be considered to be a twentieth-century "apostle of fear."

Chapters 2, 3, 4, 5, 6, and 7 begin with a short paragraph in which Germany's history during those years is briefly recounted and important aspects of Schmitt's professional and personal life are mentioned. Chapter 2 is entitled "From Normal Justice to Exceptional Law" and it covers the years 1912–1919. This is a period during which Germany went through at least three fundamental transformations—from peacetime economic power to wartime and defeat to a radical change of government. Carl Schmitt's life went through three major transformations during this period—from student to military member to the beginning of his role as a major legal and political thinker. The focus of Chap. 3 is much narrower and covers the years 1919–1923. For Germany, these years were chaotic—the formation of the Weimar government, civil unrest, and explosive inflation. Schmitt's life was comparatively comfortable—although his private life remained unsettled, he was established as a major legal thinker whose opinions carried considerable weight—even if not everyone agreed with them. Chapter 4 begins in 1924 and ends in 1926. The writings from these years are not as weighty as some of his earlier ones and they are not nearly as famous as some of his later ones. However, they are indicative of his growing reputation and they are indicative of his increasing concern about the disorder in Germany. It is in these essays that he again attacks liberalism's emphasis on the individual and criticizes parliament because of its liberal leanings. And, it is here that Schmitt begins his examination of Article 48 of the Weimar constitution and his warning about the need for "public security and order." Chapter 5 focuses on the years 1927 and part of 1928 and it reveals the tension in Schmitt's thinking regarding the relationship between law and politics. The writings from these years contain some further criticisms of parliament and democracy. The problem with the former is that it is too often the forum for endless discussions and the problem with the latter is the claim of pluralism. What Germany needed was a single leader and one to represent the people's will. Chapter 6 continues the focus on 1928 and includes 1929 and concentrates mostly on constitutional issues. This includes Schmitt's essay regarding the guardian of the constitution. But the chapter also addresses the tension between democracy's twin beliefs about freedom and equality. For Schmitt, liberalism's problem is its emphasis on the individual whereas his concern is with the people. Chapter 7 covers the years 1930–1932 and that means examining a range of Schmitt's writings. These include some rather bland legal works like *Legalität und Legitimität*, but it also includes his polemical tracts, such as *Der Begriff des Politischen*. Thus, it covers the issues of legality as well as legitimacy, and it also includes his continuing assaults on the deficiencies of liberal democracy in general and of the Weimar constitution in particular. Finally, this period seems to mark Schmitt's transition from legal scholar to party partisan and it culminates in his attacks on law and liberalism.

Chapter 8 contains three sections. In the first, I review Schmitt's account of fear and how he traces it back to Thomas Hobbes. In the second section, I show how Leo Strauss and Michael Oakeshott developed different and more liberal accounts of Hobbes' thinking. In the third section, I build upon Strauss and Oakeshott to offer a sketch of a defense of modern law and liberalism. During this time of Trump, Putin, Orban, and others, law and liberalism need a robust defense. Such a defense cannot be mounted here but one possible outline is sketched. Carl Schmitt may not have been a model citizen but he was a great scholar. This book is an attempt to trace his legal and political thinking between 1912 and 1932 and to show that his critiques of law and liberalism have continued relevance.

In this work I have mostly refrained from engaging any of the vast and mostly negative secondary literature on Carl Schmitt. I chose to ignore it because of the length of the book and because I wanted to explain Schmitt's writings during this period and not enter into debates with other interpretations. For those who would like some guidance regarding some informative works, I highly recommend *The Oxford Handbook of Carl Schmitt* edited by Jens Meierhenrich and Oliver Simons (Oxford: Oxford University Press. 2019). I have also minimized the discussion of the historical context of the period as well as biographical details of

Schmitt's life. I highly recommend Reinhard Mehring's instructive biography *Carl Schmitt: Aufstieg und Fall. Eine Biographie* (München: Beck. 2009). This is now available in English as *Carl Schmitt. A Biography*, translated by Daniel Steuer (Oxford: Polity. 2014). Finally, all translations are my own. Some of this is because some of the English translations of Schmitt's writings are not the best. My choice was predicated upon two factors: translating is a subjective task and that I have been translating German scholarship for more than 30 years. It is my hope that this book will help stimulate others to read what Schmitt actually wrote and to take seriously his criticisms of law and liberalism; that way, one might be better equipped to mount a vigorous defense of two of the most crucial pillars of modern democracy.

References

Schmitt, Carl (1988a) *Positionen und Begriffe. Im Kampf mit Weimar-Genf-Versailles. 1923–1939.* Berlin: Duncker & Humblot.

Schmitt, Carl (1988b) "Der Führer schützt das Recht." In Schmitt 1988a. 199–203.

References

2

From Normal Justice to Exceptional Law: 1912–1919

Abstract This chapter is entitled "From Normal Justice to Exceptional Law" and it covers the years 1912–1919. This is a period during which Germany went through at least three fundamental transformations—from peacetime economic power to wartime and defeat to a radical change of government. Carl Schmitt's life went through three major transformations during this period—from student to military member to the beginning of his role as a major legal and political thinker.

Keywords Justice • Power • Liberalism • Will • State

The period from 1912 to 1919 was one of change, war, and revolution in Germany. It began as a rather peaceful time but that was shattered by the war. The initial welcoming of the war and the belief in an early victory were replaced by shortages and death. The abdication of the Kaiser did not quell the growing unrest and revolutionary activities broke out in late 1918 and into 1919. Carl Schmitt's life during this period appeared to follow some of this trajectory; it began by the publication of this doctoral dissertation and then his "Habilitationschrift," but then he entered into

© The Author(s) 2020

C. Adair-Toteff, *Carl Schmitt on Law and Liberalism*, Palgrave Studies in Classical Liberalism, https://doi.org/10.1007/978-3-030-57118-4_2

military service. During that time, he seemed to swing between a sense of accomplishment and despair. He took great satisfaction in marrying Pawla Carita Dorotić but then regretted it. He had passed all of the academic requirements and seemed destined for scholarly greatness, but he frequently thought about committing suicide. Like Germany, Schmitt's life was chaotic and unpredictable.

During the period 1912–1919, Carl Schmitt published a number of writings which directly address the issue of the relationship between law and governance. Although his dissertation and his "Habilitätionsschrift" (the second dissertation which is required in Germany to teach at the university level) do not specifically mention the state of emergency nor does it contain any formal critique of liberalism, however, they do contain the seeds for his later legal and political thinking.[1] In particular, they begin to reveal his disenchantment with law and they chart his further movement away from liberalism. They show that his belief that law is political was increasing and that his opinion that the liberal state was unworkable.

But beginning in 1915, Schmitt increasingly turned to the topic of the need for extraordinary measures and to the issue of justifying dictatorial powers. Although none of these writings actually contain anything resembling his later explosive claims, they are undoubtedly important for understanding his later arguments against normal justice and modern liberalism. This chapter is relatively brief and is divided into two parts: the first which focuses on the years 1912 through 1914 and covers his writings on law, and the second which covers the period between 1915 and 1919 which focuses on his writings for the military. Both parts help demonstrate Schmitt's transition from his focus on normal justice to his preoccupation with exceptional law.

Carl Schmitt was 24 years old when he published his Strassburg dissertation, yet it reveals a remarkable sense of maturity by its choice of topic and the manner in which Schmitt approached his subject. This makes it more puzzling that Schmitt's *Gesestz und Urteil* has been largely

[1] Schmitt made this point in his 1978 note (see Schmitt 2016: VI).

neglected.[2] Schmitt dedicated the dissertation to his director Fritz van Calker and his political and juridical ideas are found in several passages of the work. If Calker tended to blend together politics and law, at least in this work Schmitt intended to keep them separate.[3] He insisted that the investigation that is found in his dissertation was a juridical one—with the clear implication that it was not concerned with politics nor with sociology. Instead, Schmitt intended to provide an answer to "The deciding question is: 'when is a legal decision correct?'" ("Die Entscheidende Frage ist die: wann ist eine richterliche Entscheidung richtig?").[4] This is not a merely theoretical issue, but goes to the heart of determining actual legal decisions. And, as Schmitt suggested, this question is not an easy one to answer despite its importance. Too often, the answer is something along the lines of it is right when the judge decides it; however, that is obviously no answer. Schmitt examines a number of possible answers.

Schmitt noted that the contemporary response to the question when is the judicial decision correct was to claim that it is correct when it is "legal" ("gesetzmäßig") (Schmitt 2016: 5). He suggests that those who believe this hold that the judge is bound to obey the law. However, this presupposes that the law is clear and that the judge actually applies the law to the specific case. In other words, the judge submits to the law.[5] In so doing, it is argued that the judge is merely following the "will of the law" ("Wille des Gesetzes") or the "will of the law giver" ("Wille des Gesetzgebers") (Schmitt 2016: 7). In this scenario the judge simply subsumes the case under the law. But Schmitt mocks the notion that the

[2] In his biography of Schmitt, Reinhard Mehring spent only two pages on it and he did not examine the work itself as much as he placed it within its historical context (Mehring 2009: 39–40). In the *Oxford Handbook of Carl Schmitt*, with the exception of bibliographic entries, the dissertation is briefly mentioned three times (Meierhenrich and Simons 2019: 29, 595, 658).

[3] Not only did Schmitt exclude politics from his discussion, he also insisted that neither psychology nor sociology has a role to play in this issue (Schmitt 2016: 15).

[4] Schmitt (2016: 1). It is important to note that Schmitt did not use the terms "legal" or "judicial" but chose the term "richterliche," "judging," or "judgelike" in order to call attention to the fact that it is a person who judges and that this is an individual rather than some general objective source. It is possible to regard Schmitt's discussion as a partial response to an ongoing debate concerning the question of "correct law" ("richtiges Recht"). The two scholars mentioned by Schmitt were Rudolf Stammler (*Die Lehre von dem richtigen Rechte*) and Hermann Kantorowicz (*Zum Lehre vom richtigen Recht*) (Schmitt 2016: 15, note 2; 16, note 1; 32).

[5] "Der Richter soll also dem Gesetz unterworfen sein" (Schmitt 2016: 7).

judge is a "subsumption machine" ("Subsumtionsmachine") or a "lawautomat" ("Gesetzautomat")[6] (Schmitt 2016: 8). The law is never completely clear and for that reason the judge cannot simply decide legal questions. Schmitt's larger point is that this scenario in no manner answers the question "when is the legal decision correct?" (Schmitt 2016: 9).

Schmitt focuses on the notion of the "will of the law" in the second chapter and he argues that it does not actually exist. Instead, the idea of a "true will" ("wahre Wille") is a "fiction" just as the belief that there is some "permanent" will. Schmitt's point is that the judge may be fair and impartial but he is still human and his will is subject to influences. That is why he refers to the will as a "hovering" will.[7] He dismisses the idea that the will contains "objective thoughts" and that it has "stabile contents" (Schmitt 2016: 33, 36). Instead, it is a "fiction" ("Fiktion") and an illusion ("Schein"). The idea that "[t]he judge should decide as the lawgiver would have decided" may very well be a "worthwhile heuristic fiction" ("wertvolle heuristische Fiktion"), but it still is a fiction.[8]

Much of the dissertation is negative, explaining what does not determine a "correct decision." However, Schmitt offers a positive answer in the final chapter which is appropriately entitled "The Correct Decision" ("Die richtige Entscheidung"). Instead of applying universal values or appealing to a general rule, Schmitt insists that the judge is bound by his time and place. He claims that "[a] judicial decision is correct today when it is taken in the same way that another judge would have decided."[9] He took pains to clarify that this does not mean that the decision is completely subjective or totally arbitrary. It is correct if it is "foreseeable and predictable."[10] Accordingly, Schmitt seeks to locate the determination of a "correct decision" between the subjective and arbitrary and the objective

[6] Later Schmitt will take issue with the claim that law is like logic or like mathematics (Schmitt 2016: 54–55, 62).

[7] The term "schwebende" is difficult to render. It does not mean hover above as it does vacillate or swing as an indication of unsteadiness or of indecision. Its point is to convey a motion between poles; perhaps the closest English translation would be "up in the air" (Schmitt 2016: 25, 30–31).

[8] "Der Richter soll so entscheiden, wie der Gesetzgeber haben würde" (Schmitt 2016: 41–42).

[9] "Eine richterliche Entscheidung ist heute dann richtig, wenn anzunehmen ist, daß ein anderer Richter ebenso entschieden hätte" (Schmitt 2016: 68; see also 75, 78, 85).

[10] "Eine richterliche Entscheidung ist dann richtig, wenn sie voraussehbar und berechenbar ist" (Schmitt 2016: 106).

and determine; he regards law as an empirical practice which is influenced by the ideas and values which the judges share (see Schmitt 2016: 112–113). What Schmitt left unsaid was that the judges who agree belong to a group who think alike and have the same values; by extension any judge who does not think the same way and have the same values is not likely to arrive at the same decision as the like-minded judges. And, what is also left unsaid is that the judge who does not arrive at the same decision is probably unfit to be a judge. Instead of liberal tolerance, Schmitt's legal view is quite restrictive. In this sense, it foretells Schmitt's later, famous distinction between "friend" and "foe."

In 1914 Schmitt first published his "Habilitationschrift," entitled *Der Wert des Staates und die Bedeutung des Einzelnen.*[11] The title is somewhat misleading because Schmitt's concern is with power and the state and not so much with the individual. This concern manifests itself rather clearly with the titles of the work's three chapters: Chapter one on "Law and Power" ("Recht und Macht"), chapter two on "The State" ("Der Staat"), and chapter three, which is the shortest, on "The Individual" ("Der Einzelne"). It is a rather defensive if not a negative work; however, it is important because it contains elements of his later legal thinking as well as his criticism of liberalism.

Schmitt begins his introduction by treating the two possible types of objections to a writing about the state and the individual: either the work is not satisfactory because of a problem with its method or it is defective because of an issue with its results (Schmitt 2015: 9). He does not think that there will be a problem with his theory but he does contend that the prevailing Neo-Kantian theory in its various forms is problematic. Schmitt spends most of the remaining part of his introduction to critiquing the works of Rudolf Stammler, Hermann Cohen, and Ernst Kantorowicz.[12] Schmitt praises them for being a part of the awakened

[11] The first edition was published by J.C.B. Mohr (Paul Siebeck) and the second by Hellerauer Verlag in 1917. The second edition utilized the book from Siebeck but changed the cover and title page. The third edition was published in 2015 by Duncker & Humblot, which is the edition used here (Schmitt 2015: 109).

[12] It is interesting to view these three thinkers through Max Weber's opinions of them. While Weber does not seem to have ever said much about Cohen, he was disgusted by Stammler's work. This is shown not only by Weber's specific 1907 critique of Stammler but also by the number of subsequent remarks. In contrast, Weber had an extremely high regard for Kantorowicz as indicated by

interest in the philosophy of law but he objects to Stammler's attempt to provide a systematic account and he is concerned by Cohen's belief in the similarity between law and mathematics (Schmitt 2015: 17–19).

The first chapter is devoted to the relationship between "law and power" ("Recht und Macht") and the thesis that law is predicated on force. This is a version of "might is right" and Schmitt's question is whether law can ever be justified by the appeal to facts. In this case, it is the claim that law is justified by the fact that the ruler has power. He insists that if law is regarded strictly as a matter of power, then it is no longer a matter of norms but of wills and purposes (Schmitt 2015: 22, 26). Yet, the fundamental understanding of law is that it is a norm. Furthermore, purposes have nothing to do with law and that there is a gap between "is and ought" ("Sein und Sollen"). Law is not a fact, but a norm (Schmitt 2015: 38–39).

The second chapter is focused on the state and Schmitt begins by discussing the relationship between law and the state. He notes that the question "which comes first?" may seem like the question of "which comes first—the chicken or the egg?" but that is misleading because law comes before the state. He suggests the confusion stems from trying to determine what a state is by examining a number of states and attempting to find what is common to all (Schmitt 2015: 44–48). Once again, the problem is methodological—trying to determine something by facts which cannot be determined by facts. The state is not a fact, but an abstraction and an ideal; thus, attempting to determine an abstraction through a "hundred incomplete things" ("hundert unvollkommende Dingen") will not yield the concept of a complete thing. Induction works in respect to facts, but not to an ideal. Schmitt compares the state to the church and specifically to the Roman Catholic Church. This is not one among many but is the sole genuine Church. In contrast, there are many different states and they can only approximate the ideal state: "civitas Dei" (Schmitt 2015: 49; see 57). Thus, law precedes the state and makes

---

his support for Kantorowicz' paper at the first conference of the Deutsche Gesellschaft für Soziologie as well as his comments on it. While it is not known whether Schmitt was aware of these opinions, given his opinion about Weber's importance, it is quite possible that he knew of them.

the state possible and the state exists in order for law to function (Schmitt 2015: 49–50, 53).

Schmitt then discusses the relationship between the law and morality and he lays part of the blame for the misguided attempt to link them to Kant. His notion of duty is found in both; unfortunately, his Neo-Kantian followers not only perpetuated this link but they strove to strengthen it. Once again, Schmitt has such leading Neo-Kantian legal philosophers such as Stammler, Cohen, and Natorp in mind (Schmitt 2015: 62–69). However, these three do not represent Neo-Kantianism in general but only the Marburg School. And, the Marburg School was not so much interested in the philosophy of law as it was in combatting Marxist influence and in establishing law as something approximating a natural science. Furthermore, the Marburg theorists strove to combine law and ethics. Yet, they are not the same but are related (Schmitt 2015: 70). And, he objects to the sociological attempt to regard the state as solely a product of society and to consider its historical manifestations (Schmitt 2015: 74). He concludes by insisting again that law has nothing to do with what has or has not happened, only with what should or should not happen.[13] Law is unconcerned with history but is focused on ethics. However, Schmitt recognized that many of his contemporaries in legal thinking were positivists of one kind or another and he was still willing to admit that they might have some grounds for emphasizing facts and experience. That is why he regarded Kelsen's early writings as valuable and significant (Schmitt 2015: 78). Nonetheless, he wanted to express his emphasis on the *philosophy of law* and not on the facts of law and he did so by mentioning Hegel's *Grundlinien der Philosophie des Rechts* and by quoting Hegel's claim that a command may not be an abstract order but needs to be a specific command.[14]

[13] Schmitt quotes with approval Heinrich Simon's comment from 1845: "The laws speak only if something should happen or should not happen, they give no foundation for the command for what really happened, and for the forbidden of what really is neglected" ("Die Gesetze sprechen nur aus, was geschehen oder nicht geschehen soll, sie geben keine Bürgschaft dafür, daß Gebotene wirklich geschieht, und das Verbotene wirklich unterlassen wird") (Schmitt 2015: 84).

[14] "Das Gesetz, muß, 'damit es Gesetz, nicht ein bloßes Gebot über haupt sey, in sich bestimmt seyn'" (Schmitt 2015: 81 and note 5).

The third chapter is devoted to the individual but almost exclusively in a negative sense. This is partially because of the liberal view that the state's monopoly on power makes it the final source for law, and the belief that the state is a combination of an impersonal mechanism and the most egoistic individualism (Schmitt 2015: 85). Schmitt does not explicitly link the individual to liberalism but the linkage hovers in the background. His initial point is that the state is frequently regarded as a "super individual" ("überindividuelle") entity but this is a mistaken assumption. The state is not an individual but an institution and even when there is a great leader, the leader is still the leader of an institution. Schmitt notes that the state can either serve the individual or the law, but not both. Yet, this apparent choice is misleading because the state must serve the law because it is the only body which has the "legal ethos" ("rechtliche Ethos") and is the only entity with the "duty towards the law" ("Pflicht zum Recht") (Schmitt 2015: 85–86).

Schmitt traces the error of the importance of the individual to the conflict among philosophers. The command to "be yourself" ("sei du selbst") is both a metaphysical statement and an ethical command. But Schmitt also points out that Being in the Platonic sense is not to be an individual but to exist as an entity. Schmitt does not blame Plato for the confusion about the importance of the individual, but he does accuse Descartes because of his "cogito ergo sum." Yes, his claim is "I think therefore I am" but Descartes was mistaken if he thought that that meant himself as an individual. It meant that he existed as an existing *being*. This is clarified if one substitutes "it thinks in me" ("es denkt in mir") instead of "I think" ("ich denke"). This is further clarified if one reflects on the phrase "die and become" ("stirb und werde"). All of these point to the insignificance of the individual and to the idea of the "self" as an ethical norm. He insists that "[t]he self in the highest sense is an ethical embodiment and not the individual person" ("Das Selbst im höchsten Sinn ist ein ethisches Gebilde, nicht der einzelne Mensch") (Schmitt 2015: 88). Schmitt turns to Kant to validate his points. First Schmitt reminds us that Kant postulates that we inhabit two worlds: the empirical world of causality and the supra-sensible realm of freedom. Second, he discusses the Kantian conception of the ethical value of the "reasonable being" ("vernünftiges Wesen"). It and not some individual has autonomy.

Furthermore, Schmitt reminds us that Kant's ethics commands us to always treat people as ends and never as means (Schmitt 2015: 89).

Schmitt contrasts the Kantian universality with the ancient distinction between the master and the slave: only the former has the capacity for law ("Rechtsfähige") whereas the latter lacks rights ("Rechtlose"). However, he makes it abundantly clear that it is not the individual master who possesses the dignity of law, but the entire class of masters (Schmitt 2015: 92–93). Returning to the concept of the state Schmitt reminds us that the state makes the individual; not that the individual makes the state (Schmitt 2015: 93). And, if there is an individual who participates in the rhythm of the state, it is not as an individual—even one so exalted to claim "le état c'est moi" but as an "instrument" ("Werkzeug"). In Canon Law, the Pope is the infallible leader because he is the "instrument" and placeholder for Christ—not because he is a specific individual (Schmitt 2015: 94–95).

As to the notion that the state gives the individual his freedom, Schmitt insists that the state does not swoop down on the individual from outside, like a "deus ex machina" but that the individual participates within the state. Accordingly, the state has the freedom and autonomy, not the individual (Schmitt 2015: 99, 101). In addition, it is wrong to speak of the will of the individual, just as Schmitt repeats his earlier criticism of the contention that there is a "will of the people" or a "volonté Générale" (Schmitt 2015: 105). Finally, the whole liberal idea of the contract theory of the state rests upon a fundamental mistake. Schmitt writes "The mistake of the contract theory was not with the construction of a contract; but rather, with the acceptance of empirical individuals as parties to a contract."[15] Schmitt concludes with two observations: first, that humans are worthy of respect *not* because they are humans. Instead, they are worthy of respect only in so far as they *can be worthy* of respect. Second, he emphasizes the insignificance of the individual by liking it to the raging rivers and the little streams which only finds the rest that they are seeking once they finally flow into the infinite sea[16] (Schmitt 2015: 108).

[15] "Der Fehler der Vertragstheore war daher nicht die Konstruktion eines Vertrages, sondern die Annahme empirischer Individuen als Vertragsparteien" (Schmitt 2015: 106).

[16] It is worth quoting the entire sentence: "In order to remain in pictures, it is easy to say that the advocate of the mediate could maintain only the source which is distant from the sea and must seek

From the earliest days of the First World War, German intellectuals wrote numerous articles in which they defended Germany from its enemies. They appealed to the German's sense of patriotism and they objected to the portraits that its enemies tried to paint of them. Germany's professors argued that Germans were not the hideous monsters that the foreign press made them appear to be and they pointed to all of the philosophical, literary, and scientific gifts that Germany's intellectuals had given to the world. Carl Schmitt chose a slightly different path. First, he published a number of brief articles and second, he did so anonymously. Third, rather than glorifying Germany, he tended to let the foreign press make their case and then he would ridicule it. From May of 1915 until February 1916 Schmitt published some twenty articles in "Die Hamburger Woche" ("The Hamburger Week"). These were propaganda articles but they still reflected Schmitt's considerable intellect and learning. Many of the articles began by referencing some French, British, or American newspaper and then making caustic comments about the people from those countries. For example, from May 1915 Schmitt begins by noting the "unconscious hatred of our enemy" ("ohnmächtige Haß unserer Feinde") and from June he writes about the hysterical response of the British to the Zeppelin airships (Schmitt 2005: 403–405). He particularly paints the French in the most unflattering light; he complains they are snobs, they are pompous, and they are stupid (Schmitt 2005: 412–414). The Americans are neither paranoid nor ignorant, but they are naïve. Schmitt refers to a man from Minnesota who will not cut his hair nor shave until the war in Europe ends (Schmitt 2005: 416). Rather than writing vociferous denunciations of Germany's enemies, Schmitt chose a more subtle method to combat foreign accounts. While these articles are intended to be reports, what Schmitt appeared to want to convey was that Germany's enemies were certainly not worthy opponents. And, once again one can begin to see the outline of his distinction between "friend and foe."

---

its way through obstacles can become a majestic river; but the immediate only sees that all the waters, the imposing rivers as well as the little streams finally end in the seas, in order to find their peace in this infinity." "Um im Bilde zu bleiben, so ließe sich noch sagen, daß der Advokat der Mittelbarkeit darauf hinweisen könnte, wie nur die Quelle, die weit vom Meere entspringt und ihren Weg durch Hindernisse suchen muß, zum majestätischen Strome werden kann, der Unmittelbarkeit aber nur sieht, daß aller Gewässer, die imposanten Ströme wie die kleine Bäche, schließlich im Meere ended, um in dessen Unendlichkeit ihre Ruhe zu finden" (Schmitt 2015: 108).

In February 1916 Schmitt gave his "Probevorlesung" ("test lecture") at Straßburg and it was then published later in the year in the *Zeitschrift für Gesamtrechtswissenschaft*. The lecture was entitled "Die Einwirkungen des Kriegszustandes auf das ordentliche strafprozessuale Verfahren" ("The Influences of the War-Conditions on the Normal Penalty-Process Procedure"). As was typical, Schmitt relied on two previous situations: the Prussian siege condition law of 1851 and the Bavarian war condition law of 1912. Because both situations were abnormal, the normal applications of penalties were changed or suspended. Now, during the winter of 1916, Schmitt maintains that the appropriate venue is questionable (Schmitt 2005: 418–419). Given the ongoing war, the question is whether criminal cases should be heard by a regular court of law or is it more appropriate for them to be held in front of a military tribunal. Civil authorities would argue that civil courts should hear such cases, whereas the military would argue that extraordinary circumstances make their court the more appropriate venue. Based upon his work for the military and his own convictions, he argues that the military court should have jurisdiction, especially in cases that involve the "interest of public security" ("Interesse der öffentlichen Sicherheit") (Schmitt 2005: 419). Schmitt argues that there are two types of cases in which the military tribunals should involve themselves in legal cases. In the first case, during the war there is the need to suspend the normal court proceedings, and in the second case where the military courts must have a dominant role, but it is limited to a particular time and a specific area (Schmitt 2005: 420). In both cases, the military is justified in determining "confinement, investigations, or confiscation of objects" ("Haft, Durchsuchung oder Beschlagnahme zum Gegenstande"). This is in order to protect the public interests thus to defend the territory (Schmitt 2005: 421, 422). It is not surprising that Schmitt argues that these measures are appropriate in judicial and political matters; it is surprising when he also includes economic instances. Now he also maintains that there is a separate province for the military courts which covers "high treason, territorial treason, murder, insurrection" ("Hochverrat, Landesverrat, Mord, Aufruhr") but he insists that the military court is not intended to replace the normal courts. Nor is he suggesting that the judges of the regular courts relinquish their judicial independence (Schmitt 2005: 423).

Schmitt moves to discuss the relationship between the military judiciary ("Militärbefehlshaber") and the attorneys for the state ("Staatsanwaltschaft") and again it appears that he is willing to grant that the latter should continue to have jurisdiction in many cases even though the state is in a state of emergency (Schmitt 2005: 426–428). Finally, he suggests that the need for military justice is limited to the need because of the state of emergency and that once that ends, military justice can return to its proper and limited jurisdiction. The normal state of justice can then take on its dominant role. Whether Schmitt really believed this is unclear, but he felt it necessary to at least make it sound as of the return to normality was possible (Schmitt 2005: 428–429).

Another of Schmitt's writings that is relevant in this time frame for the relationship between law and liberal was Schmitt's article "Recht und Macht." This was his return to one of his earlier themes and the article appeared in the first issue of 1917 of the short-lived journal *Summa. Eine Vierteljahresheft*. Once again, Schmitt's question is, does "might make right" or does "right give might"? As to the first, Schmitt notes that just as the big fish have the "right" to eat the little ones so does the member of the ruling class have the "right" to continue to keep the members of the lower class in submission. In both cases, the "right" depends upon "might." Anyone who dares to question the claim "might makes right" is no better than a "poor fool" ("armer Narr") and that in reality, all strive for power (Schmitt 2005: 432–433). In fact, Schmitt takes issue with this philosophical either/or framing and maintains that it is really a question of how it is in terms of facts in the real world; that is, what is the real relation between law and power? To put it differently, what is the relationship between law ("ought"/"Sollen") and power ("is"/"Sein")? (Schmitt 2005: 434). If law is defined as power, then law is no longer a question of norms but is an issue of "will and purpose" ("Wille und Zweck"). It is no longer a matter of juridical argumentation but is a matter of "the will of the state in its concrete factuality" ("der Wille des Staates in seiner konkreten Tatsächlichkeit") (Schmitt 2005: 435). However, scholars want to provide law with a level of dignity and so they often speak of the "good reasons" ("guten Gründen") or the "will of God" ("Willen Gottes"). However, that leads to the paradox about the big fish having the "right" to eat the little fish because we have moved from the natural world of the animal kingdom to the "human world of purposeful human action" ("zweckbewußten menschlichen Handelns") (Schmitt 2005: 436). And, that moves us from considering matters of fact to the philosophy of law and its attendant "reasonableness, enlightenment, correctness" ("Vernünftigkeit, Aufklärung, Richtigkeit") (Schmitt 2005: 437). However, there are those who want to speak only about law as fact. These are scholars who dislike abstract theories and want to focus only on facts—the legal empiricists. However, if we are restricted to only facts then there can be no law. In fact, the claims "law is only power" ("Recht ist nur Macht") and "all power is only law" ("alle Macht ist nur Recht") do not reveal their connections but display the two propositions' incompatibility. Again, when one addresses the issue concerning the purpose of law, one points to the antagonism between "is" ("Sein") and "ought" ("Sollen") (Schmitt 2005: 440–441). Schmitt does not appear to offer a concrete solution but concludes with the observation that the problem remains one of two realms—law and power (Schmitt 2005: 444).

If Schmitt was content to leave the discussion in "Recht und Macht" without determining which of the two ultimately had priority, in "Diktatur und Belagerungszustand" he appears to side with power. He published this article in 1916 in order to clarify the difference between a "dictatorship" and a "state of siege" ("Belagerungszustand"). He noted that he was primarily examining historical examples in order to provide a "legal-state study" ("Staatrechtliche Studie") (Schmitt 1995: 3). He began by asserting that in too many countries, the terms "state of siege" ("Belagerungszustand"), "state of war" ("Kriegszustand"), or "dictatorship" ("Diktatur") all appear to indicate "states of emergency" ("Ausnahmezustände"). This lumping these different states under one heading obscures the fundamental differences among them and Schmitt seeks to explain them. He does so primarily by examining some historical examples, most notably the French Revolution and the aborted revolutions in some European countries during 1830 and 1848. He claims that since the 1848 revolution the attempts to deal with political unrest have been referred to as both a state of siege and a dictatorship. However, the two terms are not the same and he justifies his claim by insisting that such an identification could not have occurred during 1789. He maintains that martial law and dictatorship would have been treated differently

(Schmitt 1995: 3–4). He contrasts it with the unrest in 1830 and 1848 because in both of these cases the separation between the executive and the legislative branches was never dissolved whereas during 1793 it was. Furthermore, the difference does not rest upon the length of time; order was restored rather quickly during 1830 and 1848 but it took much longer in 1793 (Schmitt 1995: 5–7). However, he notes that each occurrence was not likely to have happened if the French declaration of human rights had not been issued in 1789 (Schmitt 1995: 5).

This work may be short, dense, and mostly historical, but it clearly shows Schmitt attempting to clarify difficult legal concepts and to show that there are real differences between a state of siege and a state of war. In the former, the source of the unrest is from inside the state; in the latter, the source is from outside (Schmitt 1995: 4). Thus, part of the difference is that when there is a state of siege, then it is a matter for security; when there is a state of war, then it is a matter for the military. In the first case, the state is threatened by internal unrest; in the second, it is threatened by an external enemy. Thus, there is a difference between an internal state of siege and an external state of war. Schmitt clarifies the crucial difference between a state of siege/state of war and a dictatorship: that in the former the separation between the executive and legislative remains. But in a dictatorship either the legislative branch takes over the executive or the executive branch takes over the legislative branch (Schmitt 1995: 16). His concern here seems to be less with a dictatorship than it is with the military. Accordingly, the military power is relatively limited to defense. However, Schmitt is just as concerned about the dictatorship and he insists that the dictator must combine the powers of the executive and the legislative in his own hands. He approvingly quotes Charles M. Clode who wrote in *The Administration of Justice under Military and Martial Law*, "The union of Legislative, Judicial and Executive Power in one Person is the essence of Martial Law" (Schmitt 1995: 9, note 15). Schmitt's concern is with situations in which a state is threatened and the time for normal deliberations is not possible. The threat is not some vague, nebulous fear but is a "concrete, factual danger" ("*konkrete, tatsächliche Gefahr*") (Schmitt 1995: 10). Such cases of clear and present danger demand a dictator, that is, a person who has the capacity to make quick and proper decisions. Only the dictator can defend the state under such circumstances. When such extreme circumstances have passed and such extraordinary measures no longer need to be taken, then the dictator can return power to the legislative body and the state will return to normality (Schmitt 1995:20). However, Schmitt was becoming increasingly convinced that normal times would never return and that extraordinary measures would become commonplace.

Carl Schmitt's early writings and lectures do not contain the unsettling concepts and the striking phrases which are frequently found in his later and more famous works. Nonetheless, the outline of his conception of the conflict between law and liberalism is apparent. The law exists solely to ensure the security and the safety of the state and its citizens; it does not exist to guarantee liberal freedom and individual rights. Liberalism and regular law could not prevent the dislocations caused by war. The war and the revolutionary aftermath helped to reinforce Schmitt's natural fear of chaos and his increasing pessimism regarding the innate goodness of humans. The chaos that came as a result of the war, the revolution, and the counterrevolution just added to his fear of uncertainty and his doubt about safety. If liberal law was not able to guarantee order and security, then Schmitt was determined to find what could guarantee them. Carl Schmitt may have never truly believed that normal justice could have ever provided adequate security for the state, but by the middle of the war he clearly engaged in doubting it. By the end of the First World War he had lost whatever faith he had in normal justice and was embarking on justifications for exceptional law.

References

Mehring, Reinhard (2009) *Carl Schmitt: Aufstieg und Fall. Eine Biographie.* München: Beck.

Meierhenrich, Jens and Simons, Oliver, editors (2019) *The Oxford Handbook of Carl Schmitt.* Oxford: Oxford University Press.

Schmitt, Carl (2016) [1912] *Gesetz und Urteil. Eine Untersuchung zum Problem der Rechtspraxis.* München: Verlag C.H. Beck. 2., unveränderte Auflage.

Schmitt, Carl (2015) [1914] *Der Wert des Staates und die bedeutung des Einzelnen.* Berlin: Duncker & Humblot. Dritte, korrigierte Auflage.

Schmitt, Carl (2005) *Carl Schmitt. Die Militärzeit 1915 bis 1919. Tagebuch Februar bis Dezember 1915. Aufsätze und Materialien.* Herausgegeben von Ernst Hüsmert und Gerd Giesler. Berlin: Akademie Verlag.

Schmitt, Carl (1995) *Staat, Großraum, Nomos. Arbeiten aus den Jahren 1916–1969.* Herausgegeben, mit einem Vorwort und mit Anmerkungen versehen von Günter Maschke. Berlin: Duncker & Humblot.

3

Law, Politics, and Sovereignty: 1919–1923

Abstract This chapter has a narrower focus than the previous one and it covers the years 1919–1923. For Germany, these years were chaotic—the formation of the Weimar government, civil unrest, and explosive inflation. Schmitt's life was comparatively comfortable—although his private life remained unsettled, he was established as a major legal thinker whose opinions carried considerable weight—even if not everyone agreed with them.

Keywords Law • Politics • Sovereignty • Weimar • Government

When Germany admitted defeat in November 1918, it not only suffered a military disaster but underwent political, social, and economic turmoil. The Kaiser abdicated and revolutionary movements were flaring up in many German cities. The following years saw increasing turmoil: the founding of the Nazi party in 1920 and the Kapp Putsch. In 1922, Walther Rathenau was assassinated and Germany began to suffer from inflation. Inflation continued to rage the following year. In contrast, Carl Schmitt's life seemed tranquil. He was appointed professor first in Munich

© The Author(s) 2020

C. Adair-Toteff, *Carl Schmitt on Law and Liberalism*, Palgrave Studies in Classical Liberalism, https://doi.org/10.1007/978-3-030-57118-4_3

and then at Greifswald and he was becoming famous through his numerous publications. Privately, he was not calm but was fearful, a sense shared by many.

Germans had no real sense of what the future would hold for them and many were extremely anxious about what would happen in the next months and years. Carl Schmitt was one of these people; his increasing fear of chaos reinforced his commitment to guarantee public security and order. Many of his writings from the period of the beginning of 1919 until the end of 1923 were reflective of these attempts. Schmitt does not directly attack the liberal conception of law; rather, he argues for a Hobbesian notion of human nature and for a conception of the purpose of the state which is at odds with liberalism. In Schmitt's view, humans are naturally evil and the state exists to ensure that people will co-exist peacefully. Schmitt's notion of what humans are and the conception of what the state does are spelled out in varying degrees in five major books which he published between 1919 and 1923.

In September of 1924 Carl Schmitt finished an almost 30-page "Vorwort" to be added to the second edition of *Politische Romantik*. In this foreword Schmitt noted that he wrote the work during 1917 and 1918 and that it was published at the beginning of 1919. He added that since then the number of writings on the Romantics had increased substantially which had prompted him to reissue his book with the new foreword. He clarified that, like mysticism, Romanticism was being used to describe a large number of phenomena: ruins, moonshine, waterfalls, and even a mill by a stream. And, he indicated that the term was applied to various feelings: poetic, dreaming, longing, and even for such apparently contradictory feelings of homesickness and the desire for seeking out distant lands (Schmitt 1982: 27, 4–6). The sense of opposition is one of the marks of Romanticism: it seeks to withdraw into history and tradition, yet it glorifies the new and celebrates the young. Furthermore, Romantics like to claim that it is the antithesis to classicism, rationalism, and the Enlightenment, in its place are "Reformation, Revolution und Romantik" (Schmitt 1982: 6, 8, 11–13). There are at least three notions which illuminate Romanticism: the rejection of the primacy of reason, the belief in the inherent goodness of mankind, and the importance of the individual (Schmitt 1982: 5, 7, 9). While humans have always tended to have Romantic notions, Schmitt believes that it was the French Revolution of 1789 which prompted the development of the Romantic movement at the end of the eighteenth century and the beginning of the nineteenth century. It signaled the rise of a new citizenship movement, one opposed to the monarchy, nobility, and the Church. It manifested itself later with the revolutionary year of 1848 and in the later revolutionary proletariat movement (Schmitt 1982: 16). The Romantic-revolutionary movement rejected authority, objectivity, and permanence and instead embraced anarchy, subjectivity, and what Schmitt refers to as "occasion." By "occasion" he means the temporary and the impermanent and he couples this term with "subjectivism." He defines Romanticism as "subjective occasionalism" and that it prefers the fleetingness and irrationality of "I" ("Ich") over the permanence and calculability of the "objective absolute" (Schmitt 1982: 23–24). Instead of the classic form of novels in literature and of its traditional type of symphonies in music, the preferred forms for Romantics include aphorisms, poems, and lyrics. The Romantics include Rousseau and Novalis but also Baudelaire and Nietzsche. These Romantics not only inveighed against all types of tradition but they promoted an individualistic-based "Gesellschaft" (Schmitt 1982: 25–27). Schmitt had no particular reason to explain what he meant by "Gesellschaft" because most of his readers would have been familiar with Ferdinand Tönnies' distinction between "Gemeinschaft" and "Gesellschaft." For Tönnies, "Gemeinschaft" was the traditional, close-knit community of rural northern Germany. In contrast, "Gesellschaft" was the modern, individualistic, and money-driven atomistic society found in the burgeoning cities.[1]

In *Politische Romantik* Schmitt contrasts Goethe with his Romantic opponents: Schlegel and Fichte and he links him with his fellow Enlightenment thinkers Lessing and Wilhelm von Humboldt. While some of the Romantics' inclinations might be laudable, like tolerance, human rights, and individual freedom, they tended to overemphasize and transform them into a type of intolerance, excessive freedom of the individual, and a blind, tyrannical "arbitrariness" ("Willkür") (Schmitt 1982: 33–34). This is why Schmitt links Romanticism and revolution

[1] See Ferdinand Tönnies, *Gemeinschaft und Gesellschaft* (Tönnies 2019).

and he places much of the blame on Rousseau. It was Rousseau who boldly proclaimed the importance of the individual and mysticism as opposed to solidarity and the Church (Schmitt 1982: 37–38). It was Rousseau who opposed the idea of community and who fought against institutions. It was Rousseau's Romanticism which was opposed to that which was classical and what was rationalistic and to absolutism. It was Rousseau who took the 1789 idea of "individualism" and coupled it with a rejection of reality. Schmitt claimed that the word "Romantik" is derived from the German word for novel ("Roman") and he insisted that it is related to the term "fable" ("Fabel") and that it lends itself toward the fantastic. He claimed that Romanticism is the "mystical-expansive yearning" ("mystisch-expansive Drang"), a "longing for the higher" ("Sehnsucht nach dem Höheren"), the "mixture of naivety and reflection" ("Mischung von Naivität und Reflexion"), and the "dominance of the unconscious" ("Herrschaft des Unbewußten") (Schmitt 1982: 45). This is not the longing of the Romantic but is also the longing of the "political romantic"—one who approaches politics from the Romantic point of view.

Schmitt begins the chapter "Die Äussere Situation" with a reference to Friedrich Schlegel. Schlegel had insisted that the great tendencies of the century were embodied in Goethe's *Wilhelm Meister,* Fichte's *Wissenschaftslehre*, and the French Revolution. Schmitt had no doubt that Schlegel was correct about all three, but what he wants to concentrate on is the political tendencies found in the French Revolution (Schmitt 1982: 53–54). Although Schlegel was an enthusiastic supporter of the revolution, he rapidly grew disillusioned with it. He objected to its ascetic idealism and its rejection of worldly pleasures and political reality. Schmitt then links Schlegel to Adam Müller who was at one time associated with the Viennese regime. Like Schlegel, Müller rejected his early enthusiasm for the French Revolution and became increasingly more conservative (Schmitt 1982: 61–66). It is not totally clear why Müller was so important for Schmitt except that he embodied the type of individual who became disillusioned with the radical individualism of Romanticism and its rejection of authority and tradition. Müller also serves as a conservative political thinker in the enlightened Prussia during the Napoleonic Wars. Furthermore, Prussia was Protestant but Austria was Catholic and Schmitt concluded this chapter with the declaration "Catholicism is not

Romantic" ("Der Katholizismus ist nicht Romantisches") (Schmitt 1982: 76).

The second chapter is entitled "Die Struktur des romantischen Geistes" and it contains two sections. The first carries the title "La recherche de la Réalité" and there is no explicit explanation why Schmitt chose to put it in French. A hint comes with his claim that the modern "spiritual situation" ("Geistige Situation") cannot be divorced from its history and that there were two fundamental historical shifts. One was Copernicus' astronomical revolution where he demonstrated that rather than being geocentric, the reality is heliocentric. The other was the Cartesian epistemological revolution in which he argued that knowledge has to begin with the cogito. Whereas Copernicus shattered the traditional view of the planetary system, Descartes destroyed the belief in an independent metaphysics (Schmitt 1982: 77–78). What resulted was the tension between poles: "thinking" and "being," "concept" and "reality," "spirit" and "nature," and "subject" and "object." However, the Cartesian emphasis on the knowing subject continued with Kant's Transcendental Idealism and then into Fichte's conception of the "absolute I" ("absolutes Ich"). Fichte's "not I" ("nicht Ich") was fundamentally nothing but pure negation, and a rejection of the philosophical belief in rationalism. Instead, there was the Romantic disavowal of "loveless wisdom" ("liebeleere Weisheit"). While there was a continuation toward abstract reason as found in parts of Spinoza's thinking and more so in Hegel's philosophy, there was far more of an emphasis on the individual and the devaluation of the external world. The outside world was regarded as a "mere perception" ("bloße Wahrnehmung") and in its stead was either an "anti-philosophical mysticism" or an "organic" philosophy of nature (Schmitt 1982: 78–81). Schmitt suggests that there has been a four-stage movement beginning with the philosophical stage which was replaced by the mystical-religious one. That stage was followed by a historical-traditional stage but has been superseded by the final emotional-aesthetic stage. The emphasis throughout these four stages has been on the individual and his feelings. The result was that "[t]he highest and most certain reality of the old metaphysic, the transcendent God, was replaced."[2] The ancient philosophical search for the abstract and universal was replaced by the concrete and singular; even with the concept of contract in political theory, the emphasis was on the individual. The result was the increasing belief in human egoism, which is nothing but "a wild will to power" ("ein rasender Wille zur Macht") and a new religion glorifying the individual. There is no doubt that Schmitt was convinced that his readers would connect this with Nietzsche's glorification of the human individual and his concern with the "Wille zur Macht." And, while Schmitt insisted that "no God, no king" ("kein Gott, kein König") was found in the "open atheism" of 1793, it was also found in the Nietzschean philosophy of 1883 (Schmitt 1982: 84, 87–89). The new Romantic religion rejected boundaries and limitations; its "revolutionary limitlessness" ("revolutionären Schrankenlosigkeit") rejected history (Schmitt 1982: 90). Instead, there was the sovereign "I," a world-creating Romantic ego. Romanticism began as the struggle of the young against the old but it transformed itself into the fight between possibility and reality and the search for new ideals. Definitions were obsolete because they were dead mechanical things; the new "reality" was self-created irrationality (Schmitt 1982: 96–99). Whereas the medieval mystic sought to lose himself in the mystical union with God, the modern Romantic dismissed God as unimportant in favor of the individual. The community was no longer conceived of something larger than the individual; rather, it was regarded as a bigger individual. The emphasis was not so much on the abstract state but on the immediate "Volk." Instead of praising the education of reading and writing, the emphasis was on naïve and sentimental poetry (Schmitt 1982: 100–102). History was regarded as irrelevant; the past was important only because it contained the innocent primitive people. The Romantic sought refuge in the view of the Middle Ages, but really longed for the Golden Age of the primitive good men who inhabited the now lost paradise (Schmitt 1982: 104). Even the modern philosophy of nature was not a study of nature as

[2] "Die höchste und sicherste Realität der alten Metaphysik, der transzendente Gott, war beseitigt" (Schmitt 1982: 86).

it is, but as it ought to be—a "nature in the higher style" ("Natur im hohen Stil"). In effect, "[t]he will to reality ended in the will to illusion."[3]

While the second section of the chapter contains some repetition from the first, "Die Occasionalistische Strukture der Romantik" does contain a number of new points. Schmitt repeats his claim that "ontological thinking" has been replaced by subjective individualism (Schmitt 1982: 115). However, he also claims that there are two modern "demiurges": humanity and history, but his emphasis here is primarily on the latter. He notes that throughout history, historians sought to link effect back to cause; now that is rejected and has been replaced in Romantic thinking by focusing simply on an occasion (Schmitt 1982: 118–119, 123). Once again, Schmitt returns to the history of philosophy and to the problem of the relation between two distinctly different substances: mind and body. He reminds us that once again philosophers have sought to bring together two contradictory phenomena into a "higher third" ("höheren Dritte") and this was sometimes regarded as God and other times as the state (Schmitt 1982: 128–129, see also 162–163). Yet, Schmitt's larger point is that this attempt was regarded as a type of evasion of reality and he insists that the Romantic sought to replace reality with a better illusion. Rather than approaching reality as something objective, the Romantic retreats into ones' self and attempts to create his own "reality." Schmitt provides a table of opposites:

Positive	Negative
Living	Dynamic-Mechanistic-mathematical
Organic	Anorganic
Real or true	Surrogate (illusion, deceit)
Sustaining	Destroying
Historical	Arbitrary
Fixed	Chaotic
Peaceful	Party, polemical
Legitimate	Revolutionary
Christian	Pagan
Class-corporation	Absolute-central

Schmitt (1982: 144)

[3] "Der Wille zur Realität endete im Wille zum Schein" (Schmitt 1982: 113).

However, Schmitt does not expand upon this table nor does he explain how some of these seem to fall into the traditional rationalism while others are Romantic. What he does do is conclude this section by insisting once again that the defining characteristic of the Romantic is the preoccupation with subjective emotion and artistic impulses (Schmitt 1982: 147–151).

Up to this point Schmitt's concern was with the philosophy of Romanticism, but in the final chapter his interest shifts to the politics of Romanticism; this is clearly signaled by the fact that this chapter shared its title with the book: *Politische Romantik* (Schmitt 1982: 153). It is also signaled by his focus on the political revolution of 1789 and its influence on Europe during the next several decades. The French Revolution gave rise to a number of new impulses but most of them can be classified under the heading of a new life of spirit. This new life of spirit was intended to overcome the dead universalism of rationalism and even Kant's philosophy was rejected as having suffered from most of the same defects of the previous incarnations of rationalism. The new spirit of life was found in Hölderlin's *Hyperion*, Novalis' "Europa und die Christenheit," Hegel's youthful "Geist des Christentums und sein Schicksal," and in the various philosophical fragments of Schleiermacher and Schlegel. Schmitt clarified that "[t]he new feeling for life expressed itself in poems, novels, and fragments."[4] And, he maintained that this new spirit was found in Schlegel's 1804 lectures on the feeling of love and faithfulness (Schmitt 1982: 158). Schlegel's organic philosophy was not a philosophy of thought but of feeling: "heart, inclination, feeling" ("Herz, Neigung, Gefühl"), and like Romantic philosophy in general it had no real use for history (Schmitt 1982: 159, 166). The only historically important occasion was the French Revolution because it set in motion the liberation from the sterile, traditional chains of church and state (Schmitt 1982: 169–170). For the Romantic, the state should be regarded as a work of art, a manifestation of the individual writ large (Schmitt 1982: 172–173, 185, 196). Schmitt repeats many of these same points in the appendix on David Friedrich Strauss. The Romantic regards Christianity as something more or less negative because it became an institution just like the state.

[4] "Das neue Lebensgefühl äußerte sich in Gedichte, Romanen, Fragmenten" (Schmitt 1982: 156).

If it has any positive value, it lies in its early years when it represented something new. The defining turning point is again the French Revolution because it freed people from the mechanistic rationalism and allowed them to engage in poetic expression (see Schmitt 1982: 216). Thus, political philosophy is replaced by a philosophical aesthetics; rather than being concerned with the actual well-being of its citizens, its concern is with the dreams of the future—an illusion where everyone is equal and free (Schmitt 1982: 225–227). This may be a future dream, but for Schmitt it is only an illusion and a very dangerous one.

Politische Romantik was a cautionary tale; Schmitt warned about the human inclination to indulge in Romantic fantasies rather than facing cold reality. This is somewhat strange given Schmitt's own predilection to fantasy and his appreciation of myth. Both of these notions will surface later in his book on Hobbes. In *Politische Romantik* Hobbes is only mentioned twice: once in reference to Hobbes' rejection of "abstract rationalism" and "concrete materialism" in favor of a type of phenomenalism and its emphasis on perception (Schmitt 1982: 80–81), and once regarding the evil nature of human beings and the war of all against all ("Kampf aller mit allen") (Schmitt 1982: 83). However, Schmitt was implicitly following Hobbes with his critique of rationalism.

In 1921, Schmitt published *Die Diktatur. Von den Anfängen des modernen Souveränitätsgedankens bis zum proletarischen Klassenkampf* and its title is a clear reference to some of his wartime publications. It not only referenced the need for someone in authority who can make quick decisions but hinted at the importance of the question of sovereignty. Both will remind readers of Hobbes, but in *Diktatur* Hobbes himself has yet to take on a major role. There are few mentions of him and these are mainly comments linking him to others who shared the view that man is naturally evil (Schmitt 1964: 9–10). Yet, there is a pervasive sense of fear of chaos and that only a dictator can save the country. This is evident in the "Vorbemerkung" to the first edition in which Schmitt noted how the chaos of the Russian Revolution of 1917 prompted interest in the notion of the dictator. However, Schmitt added that the emphasis on the "dictatorship of the proletariat" obscured the importance of the concept of the dictator and its history. His *Dikatur* was intended not just to rectify this omission; it was also to justify the need for one in contemporary Germany

(Schmitt 1964: XIII–XVIII). For the purposes here, Schmitt's major appendix on Wallerstein can be omitted in its entirety and the first section on theory and the later section on the French Revolution can be dealt with quickly. While all three are of interest to historians, they are not particularly relevant to Schmitt's focus on order and security.

Schmitt begins *Die Diktatur* as he often does by appealing to history and to etymology. While he is often correct historically, he is not always justified in his linguistic claims. Here, he maintains that the word "dictator" comes from the word "dictatura"—to dictate (Schmitt 1964: 1, 4 and footnotes 4 and 5). This claim is somewhat questionable but his claim that the term is Roman is beyond doubt. For the Romans, the dictator was an exceptional magistrate and he had the extraordinary task to defend the state in dangerous times (Schmitt 1964: 1, 5). Schmitt adds that dangerous times may be more extensive than the six months that the Romans gave the magistrate and he appeals to a list of thinkers who regarded humans as inherently bad. Men were by nature evil; they are beasts ("Bestie") and rabble ("Pöbel"). The thinkers included Machiavelli, Luther, and Hobbes (Schmitt 1964: 9). Rather than thinking of the modern state as a neutral and technical apparatus, Schmitt prompts the reader to consider the state as an expression of sovereignty. If one regards the natural condition as a war of all against all, then the state comes into being out of the need to protect one against others. It is the need for security which led Hobbes to his notion of the absolute sovereign who safeguards the peace and security of all of his subjects. It is the absolute sovereign who has the power to determine not only mundane issues such as what is yours and what is mine; he also has the power to determine what is considered good and what is regarded as evil. In other words, the decisive power of Hobbes' sovereign is his power to decide and that makes him a dictator (Schmitt 1964: 21–22).

What makes Schmitt's mention of Hobbes so noteworthy is his belief that what Hobbes believed about the need for an absolute sovereign still applies today and that is because the modern state is not a normal state but is the "state of emergency" ("Ausnahmezustand"); hence the law cannot be regarded as anything but a command—an order ("Befehl") and it is the sovereign who gives orders (Schmitt 1964: 22–24). Much of the remainder of the first chapter is given over to a discussion of the Roman dictator who was limited in the time he was given full control and the modern notion of the sovereign and his life-time rule. This leads to Schmitt's distinction between a commissar dictatorship and a sovereign one. Schmitt admits that this distinction is based upon Bodin's discussion, but here Schmitt suggests that this distinction is one without much of a difference because Bodin made it in relation to the French monarchy. Thus, the commissar was not so much limited in time but was the instrument of the monarch (Schmitt 1964: 31–39).

The two chapters which are of major interest here are chapters four and six. Chapter four is on the concept of the sovereign dictator and chapter six is about the role the dictator has during a state of emergency. What underlies the concept of the sovereign dictator is the opposition between law and authority. Legislators have law but they have no power, hence no authority. In contrast, the dictator has power, but has no law. This is the opposition between "powerless law" ("machtlose Recht") and "lawless power" ("rechtlose Macht") (Schmitt 1964: 126). It is this background that is present in Schmitt's concept of the sovereign dictator. However, Schmitt begins the chapter by noting that the medieval notion of sovereign is not the same as the modern one and that is because the medieval sovereign was granted authority by God through the Church. This theological basis for sovereignty was replaced in England in 1647 with the "Agreement of the People." This was the first draft of the modern conception of a democratic constitution, but it led to Cromwell's dictatorship (Schmitt 1964: 127–130). Cromwell insisted it was necessary to suspend the constitution in order to safeguard peace and security. The people could not guarantee order so Cromwell insisted that he received his authority from God (Schmitt 1964: 134–135). For Schmitt, security and order can be found only in a state that is a unity—divergency of opinions leads to disorder, so it is imperative that the state has one voice and one will. It is under this circumstance that the state can continue to exist. Once again Schmitt believes that the history of the French Revolution is instructive—the competing voices led to chaos and it was only with Napoleon's efforts that order was restored (Schmitt 1964: 142–148, 154, 165–166).

The final chapter is focused on the role of the dictator in reestablishing "legal order and security" ("rechtliche Ordnung und Sicherheit") (Schmitt

1964: 169). As he had written during the war, here again Schmitt discusses how the military is the only instrument to ensure tranquility during states of emergency. During such states, the normal legal order ceases to function; thus, it falls to the dictator to declare a national emergency and employ all necessary measures to restore calm and to guarantee safety (Schmitt 1964: 170–175, 179, 182). That means that the constitution is suspended and the rights of the citizens are reduced during the duration of the "state of siege" ("Belagerungszustand") (Schmitt 1964: 186–188). And, that means that the issue of sovereignty becomes one of unlimited power of the state—supreme power. This issue repeated itself in the French Revolution of 1830–1832 and again in the Revolution of 1848 (Schmitt 1964: 195–197). This brings Schmitt to his concluding points about the current situation in Germany.

Germany instituted its new constitution in August of 1919 and it enumerated the rights and duties of all of its citizens. The Weimar constitution would be of increasing interest to Schmitt and in particular on a specific article. This article was Article 48 and it dealt with the state of emergency. It will continue to be a major focus of this book so it is worthwhile now to give it in full.

> When a state cannot fulfill its duties in accordance with the constitution of the Reich or laws of the Reich, then the Reich President can fulfill them with the help of the power of arms.
>
> If the public security and order of the German Reich is disturbed or threatened, the President of the Reich will restore the public security and order through the necessary means, including with the help of armed power.
>
> (Wenn ein Land die ihm nach der Reichsverfassung oder den Reichsgesetzen obliegen Pflichten nicht erfüllt, kann der Reichspräsident es dazu mit Hilfe der bewaffeneten Macht.
>
> Der Reichspräsident kann, wenn im Deutschen Reiche die öffentliche Sicherheit und Ordnung erheblich gestört oder gefährdet wird, die zur Wiederherstellung der öffentliche Sicherheit und Ordnung nötigen Maßnahmen treffen, erforderlichenfalls mit Hilfe der bewaffeneten Macht einschreiten.)

Here Schmitt does not provide a complete, critical account of Article 48; instead, he focuses on one important contradiction. The Article concludes by indicating that the government can set aside either partially or completely the right to personal freedom, the right to living quarters, the right to privacy in correspondence, the right to freedom of the press, the right to associate, and the right to vote. The contradiction is how can the government be limited in any way in these matters when it has the complete right to determine life or death (Schmitt 1964: 199–200). Schmitt's implicit point is that Article 48, as well as most of the Weimar constitution, is so filled with qualifications and contradictions that it is not only a rather meaningless document, but a dangerous one. Legal rules may be effective during normal times, but they are ineffectual during abnormal ones. Hobbes was right: "Authority, not truth make laws" (Schmitt 1964: 21).

Schmitt's work *Politische Theologie* has a rather unusual history because it appeared in two versions. The first one was published in 1922 as an article in the two-volume book which honored the memory of Max Weber (Schmitt 1923). It carried the title "Soziologie des Souveränitätsbegriffes und politische Theologie," yet a reading of it reveals that it had almost nothing to do with sociology but was a continuation of Schmitt's thinking about dictators. The second version was the book which was published the following year. Schmitt dropped the pretense of being a sociological work and it simply carried the title *Politische Theologie.* A comparison between the two versions shows that the book version carries a subtitle "Vier Kapitele zur Lehre von der Souveränität" which indicated that there were four chapters instead of the three of the earlier, essay version. The fourth chapter was the final one and it was primarily focused on the counterrevolutionary doctrine of the state. This chapter also contained several antitheses which included the opposition between the belief in man being naturally good and the one maintaining that man was inherently bad. For some, like Rousseau, man was inherently good and that it was the chains of civilization that corrupted him. Schmitt did not believe it necessary to spend any real effort in debunking Rousseau's contention. The Enlightenment thinkers also contended that man was inherently bad; however, they believed that he could be educated and made better. This belief was in accordance with the Enlightenment belief in progress and reason. Schmitt does not directly attack this conception; rather, he notes that the Enlightenment thinkers despised the Roman Catholic Church because of its emphasis on authority and tradition. In this, the Enlightenment thinkers were in accord with the anarchists who regarded the Church as nothing better than the Church of the Grand Inquisitors (Schmitt 2015: 59–62). This, of course, is a misleading account of the Church and is a misrepresentation of liberalism. Georg Jellinek had argued that men had a universal right to freedom and that meant the ability to participate in democratic discussions. However, democratic discussions can occur during normal times when there is no need for a speedy decision. In normal times citizens and law makers can engage in lengthy deliberations and have leisurely discussions—and there is usually little or no harm to the existing political order. However, Schmitt is preoccupied with abnormal times so he addresses the opposition between order and chaos. He argued that in normal times there is order but these were not normal times but were chaotic. Hence, there was no time for discussions, but it was certainly the right time for a dictator because a "[d]ictatorship is the opposite to discussion" ("Diktatur ist der Gegensatz zur Diskussion") (Schmitt 2015: 66–67). And, this brings up the issue that was found in both the title of the essay version as well as the subtitle of the book version of *Politische Theologie*—namely the fundamental issue of sovereignty.

Schmitt had begun both versions with the assertion "[t]he sovereign is the one who decides on the state of emergency" ("Souverän ist, wer über den Aufnahmezustand entscheidet") (Schmitt 1923: 5, 2015: 11). This bold assertion recalls Schmitt's opening lines in his 1912 dissertation in two ways: first, the similar high degree of provocation, and second, the identical stress on the need for decisions (Schmitt 2016: 1). Rather than attempting to follow Schmitt's stages of execution, it may be clearer to examine his discussion regarding sovereignty in different stages. The focus of the second chapter is on the definitions of sovereignty offered by Hans Kelsen and others and how, in Schmitt's opinion, they fail. Their definition is juridical and deals with norms; however, Schmitt insists that the "Aufnahmezustand" is extraordinary and exists outside of the normal course of laws. Kelsen and the others want to regard the state as a rational, purposeful business and consider calculability to be a crucial part of it (Schmitt 2016: 27–30, 34, 69). They make the additional error in following Locke who believed that "[t]he Law gives authority." Instead, they should have followed Hobbes who insisted in *Leviathan* that "Autoritas, non veritas facit legim." Thus, rather than legal truths giving rise to authority, it is authority which delivers laws (Schmitt 2016: 38–39). While laws may work during normal times, what is needed during an extraordinary situation is the power of decision. And, that brings us back to Schmitt's opening challenge about who makes the decision about the state of emergency and why. His answer is that the sovereign is the single individual who has the sole authority to determine when there is a state of emergency and that the sovereign must have the authority because during states emergency, a decision must be made immediately to ensure public order and security. Schmitt devotes much of *Politische Theologie* to advancing these positions.

Unlike most laws, the notion of sovereignty is not a regular type of law but is a "Grenzbegriff." This compound noun is difficult to render because of its complexity, "Begriff" is not problematic and it is almost always rendered as "concept." "Grenz," however, is problematic because it can be translated as "limit" or "boundary." From Schmitt's usage it can be either—it is a limiting concept or it can be one about a boundary, but in either case it is not a typical legal term. It is not a normal juridical term because it does not apply to a "normal case" ("Normalfall") but to a "borderline case" ("Grenzfall"). Normal laws cannot be applied to abnormal cases and during a state of emergency ("Aufnahmezustand") because they require a decision in the most eminent sense. That is because a state of emergency is declared when the public order and security is under attack, but the highest level of emergency is demanded when the state itself is threatened (Schmitt 2016: 13–14). To explain that the state of emergency demands a sovereign, Schmitt sketches a historical account of the development of the concept of sovereignty.

Schmitt repeats his earlier claim in *Die Diktatur* that the doctrine of sovereignty began with Jean Bodin. In the book *On Sovereignty* Bodin defined sovereignty as the "absolute and perpetual power" (Bodin 2009: 65). It is "absolute" because it allows no exceptions or limitations and it is "perpetual" because it cannot be bound by any time frame. The sovereign also differs from all others, including political leaders because only he is not subject to any one else and that he is not bound by any laws (Bodin 2009: 81). Bodin also discusses how the sovereign makes laws, conducts war, pardons criminals, and institutes coinage but Schmitt is uninterested in these matters. What he is interested is in the extraordinary power which makes a "sovereign majesty" (Bodin 2009: 87; Schmitt 2016: 15–16). In particular, his concern is with matters which are necessary and urgent and require an immediate decision—one that can be rendered only by the sovereign (Schmitt 2016: 15). Schmitt recognizes that public order and security can be threatened by relatively normal actions and that these cases can be addressed by appealing to regular laws. However, in a situation in which the state is threatened then normal laws are ineffectual. As a result, the sovereign is required to make an immediate and binding decision (Schmitt 2016: 16–17). Furthermore, not every "police emergency situation or emergency ordering" ("polizeiliche Notstandmaßnahme oder Notverordnung") is a "state of emergency" ("Ausnahmezustand") and when they are not, normal laws are sufficient. When it is a genuine state of emergency then normal laws are suspended. And, it is the sovereign who is solely responsible to determine whether it is a genuine state of emergency (Schmitt 2016: 18–19). Schmitt begins to clarify why he is so preoccupied with the state of emergency. He notes that this differs from normal chaos and traditional anarchy because normal cases prove nothing; the "exception" ("Ausnahme") proves everything and that makes the exceptional more interesting than the general. Quoting from Gerhard Anschütz, it is here that the law of the state ends ("Das Staatsrecht hört hier auf") (Schmitt 2016: 20–21).

In the modern history of law, the state of emergency was problematic. Schmitt noted that for Locke, it was an incommensurable, and for Kant, "emergency law" ("Notrecht") was not law (Schmitt 2016: 20). That is because the state of emergency demands a decision and neither Locke nor Kant believed in decisionism. The classical representative of decisionism was of course Hobbes (Schmitt 2016: 39). Although Schmitt does not mention it here, he later devoted a small book to Hobbes' theological basis for his notion of the Leviathan. But, in the beginning of the third chapter of *Politische Theologie* he insists that the concepts in the modern doctrine of the state are secularized theological concepts: the all-powerful God has been changed into the omnipotent law giver and the notion of the miracle has been transformed in to the state of emergency (Schmitt 2016: 43–44). Schmitt credits Kelsen for having recognized the methodological affinity between theology and jurisprudence but faults him for seeking to link normative law-likeness to natural law-likeness and for his inclination toward normalcy and democracy (Schmitt 2016: 46–47). He suggests that these flaws hindered Kelsen from fully appreciating the relationship between law and theology. Schmitt insisted that the dogma that laws were divine decrees was replaced by a doctrine of earthly laws and that the notion of God as divine sovereign was changed into a mundane one. And, just as God had created the world and determined its laws, the founders of the state created it and its judiciary (Schmitt 2016: 51–54). But the Enlightenment thinkers gave rise to revolution and that produced the early nineteenth-century counterrevolution. It was the great Catholic thinker Donoso Cortés who recognized both that metaphysics was at the basis of all politics and that there was no longer any royalism because there was no longer a king. As a result, there was no longer any basis for legitimacy and the single result was the dictator and decisionism. That leads Schmitt back to Hobbes and his claim "Autoritas, non veritas facit legem" (Schmitt 2016: 54–55). It is not truth and democracy which prevails; rather, it is authority and the sovereign dictator. And, Schmitt defends this claim more fully in a work that he published in 1923.

The work is *Die geistesgeschichtliche Lage des heutigen Parlamentarismus* and it is devoted to showing that many aspects of liberal thinking are wrong. In this book Schmitt insists that it is necessary to address a number of aspects of modern political thinking, among which are democracy, liberalism, individualism, and rationalism (Schmitt 1996: 30). Yet, it is worth mentioning that of the four sections in the book, only the first two deal directly with liberalism and democracy. The third concerns the belief in rationalism which led from Hegel to Marx and its conviction of "iron necessity" ("eiserne Notwendigkeit"). The "naïve rationalism" of the Enlightenment was transformed into the "philosophy with the sabre" (Schmitt 1996: 64, 66, 73, 76). The fourth section builds upon the rationalist myth and Schmitt argues that it leads to the Marxist dictatorship of the proletariat. In other words, rationalism does not lead to freedom, as Hegel believed; it ends in the irrational dictatorship of communism (Schmitt 1996: 84–89).

The first two sections are the ones of interest here: the first is on the relationship between democracy and parliament while the second is on the principles of parliament. Schmitt again begins by looking at history and notes that during the nineteenth century it seemed that democracy was dominating the West—no western European country could resist the expansion of democratic ideas and institutions. It was the struggle between old and new and it was readily apparent that this struggle was ending with the victory of new democracy over the old monarchies. But Schmitt appears to begin the nineteenth century with the year 1789. He insisted that the French Revolution released the "flood of democracy" which no dam could withhold and that it swept away not just the Old World but the New One as well. He mentioned how Alexis de Tocqueville observed American democracy and reported its success back in France. Schmitt suggested that Tocqueville's book contributed to the renewal of interest in democracy in France and the belief in the natural goodness of people (Schmitt 1996: 30–32). Furthermore, Schmitt credits the French with combining the ideas of democracy, freedom, and liberalism, but notes that it was Rousseau who emphasized the notion of the will of the people. Schmitt believes that the kernel of democratic thinking is the identity of the law and the will of the people, but that the real issue is determining what the will of the people is (Schmitt 1996: 34–37). Furthermore, there is the question of how radical democracy reflects the will of all people—including women. But what he objects to is the doctrine that holds that dictatorship is the opposite of democracy because the former can represent the will of the people just as well as democracy does. And, he maintains that democracy does not necessarily involve parliament (Schmitt 1996: 37–41).

Section two sets out the principles of parliament and Schmitt begins by briefly discussing the struggle between what represents the will of the people and the monarchy. Previously, the monarch could maintain that he represented the will of the people or simply discount it as being unimportant or simply irrelevant, but with the advent of democracy, the voice of the people shifted from the monarchy to parliament (Schmitt 1996: 41). However, Schmitt takes issue with the notion that parliament can represent the people by arguing first that parliament does not represent all of the people and second that members of parliament are elected for a limited period of time. Thus, members of parliament are members of a small class and that they are limited in the amount of time they can legally claim to represent the people (Schmitt 1996: 42–43).

Schmitt turns his attention to the notion of liberalism and insists that it is crucial to regard it as a complete metaphysical system. It is a system that claims systematic freedom: a belief in the free economic individual who has the freedom to enter into contracts, the freedom to trade, and the freedom of competition. That there may be a fuller social harmony and an improvement in the distribution of wealth are simply secondary results of the "general liberal principle" ("allgemein liberales Prinzip") (Schmitt 1996: 45). The remainder of this section is composed of a critique of liberalism and its various beliefs.

First is the belief that liberalism and democracy are identical. They are not because liberalism is a metaphysical system and democracy is a political form. Second is the belief that liberalism safeguards a number of freedoms: freedom of speech, freedom of the press, freedom of assembly, and freedom of discussion. Schmitt suggests that these are simply various manifestations of one type of freedom—the freedom of opinion. And, the issue of freedom of opinion takes Schmitt to the issue of public opinion ("öffentliche Meinung"). Schmitt again traces this belief in public opinion back to the Enlightenment and its devotion to reason. The Enlightenment held that where there was freedom of the press there could be no abuse of power. That is because the Enlightenment thinkers believed in the pure power of reason, and as long as people know the truth, they would act accordingly. However, public opinion was shown to be open to being molded and that various forces would engage in ways to shape it favorably to their own sides (Schmitt 1996: 47–50). Schmitt noted that the difference in opinion did not exist just in public, but also in parliament, and that both implied discussions—in fact, interminable and even eternal discussions. And, this leads to Schmitt's distinction between parliament and the executive: the former focuses on laws and truth; the latter is involved with authority and orders. Members of parliament deliberate; the executive acts (Schmitt 1996: 55–56). Thus, the two liberal principles of individual freedom and collective deliberation actually conflict and result in paralysis. Parliament is not the rational safeguard that its liberal defenders maintain that it is; rather, the only political form which can unify and act is the decisionist leader—the genuine (non-Marxist) dictator (Schmitt 1996: 57–62).

The final book to be considered in this chapter may not seem to be relevant. *Römischer Katholizismus und politische Form* begins and ends with Schmitt's denunciation of the anti-Catholic movements. However, as the second part of the title suggests, he regards Catholicism as much a political force as he does a theological one. In fact, he considers Roman Catholicism to be a far superior political-theological movement than he considers Protestantism. Moreover, *Römischer Katholizismus und politische Form* contains a massive critique of modern industrial society. However, Schmitt does not suggest a retreat to some mythical golden age; rather, he directs us to regard Roman Catholicism as the leading authority to lead us in these difficult times.

In many respects Schmitt follows Max Weber's account of Protestantism and its role in the development of modern capitalism. Schmitt agrees with Weber's claim that the Protestants' single-minded devotion to work is intended to glorify God. And, he agrees with Weber that the theological foundation was replaced by a moral one and he also agrees that that moral foundation has fallen away in modern industrial capitalism. Finally, he agrees that the future seems bleak because of the emphasis on technique and calculability has replaced humanity's devotion to religion. Schmitt contends that machines dominate modern life and they have contributed to an irrational consumerism (Schmitt 2002: 19, 25, 33–34, 41). And, he believes that this consumerism has displaced religious belief. Schmitt seeks to show that religion should regain its rightful place as authority and he does so by examining some of the core tenets of modern criticism of Roman Catholicism. Schmitt agrees with Rudolph Sohm that the Catholic Church embraces Canon Law; however, whereas Sohm argued that Catholic Canon Law is at odds with the charismatic authority of early Protestantism, Schmitt insists that it is the Catholic emphasis on hierarchy which makes it a powerful authority for modernity (Schmitt 2002: 49, 53–54).

Schmitt argues that Roman Catholicism embodies what is good in human kind: it is able to overcome all kinds of oppositions, including reason and faith, material and spirit, mechanism and nature, bad and good (Schmitt 2002: 11, 19). Drawing on his earlier works, Schmitt traces how Protestantism gave rise to the French Revolution and to the twin movements of Romanticism and capitalism. And, he insists again that despite the apparent opposition, capitalism and communism are actually quite similar. Both emphasize economics and both reject traditional authority (Schmitt 2002: 60). And, both have a distrust, if not a hatred, of Roman Catholicism.

Yet, it is Roman Catholicism that has the right type of reason, the right type of brotherhood, and the right type of politics. It has the right type of reason because it is not the irrational rationality of capitalism but is balanced by faith. It has the right type of brotherhood because it is not the secular brotherhood of communism but is a brotherhood founded on faith. Finally, it is the right type of politics because instead of paying lip service to the notion of representation, it is founded on the idea of the Pope as the representative of Christ (Schmitt 2002: 2336). Capitalism and communism reject tradition and embrace an "iron and glassy crystal," yet Catholicism is built upon tradition and believes in the warmth of nature (Schmitt 2002: 16, 46). Finally, Schmitt maintains that capitalism's exclusive concern with economics means that it is no longer concerned with politics. In contrast, Catholicism is in the "eminent sense" political (Schmitt 2002: 27). And, it is the Catholic concern with humanity which prompts individuals as different as Bismarck and Dostoevsky to paint Roman Catholicism in the darkest colors—the former in believing it to be a threat to the nation and the latter as the Grand Inquisitor (Schmitt 2002: 5, 55). Yet, it is the Church with its essential humanity, its true justice, and its real goal of peace which should be regarded as the authentic authority on earth (Schmitt 2002: 44, 49–50, 65).

Throughout the years 1919–1923, Schmitt confronted the problem of the lack of genuine authority. He was convinced by the continual fighting between the Left and the Right that the successive Weimar governments lacked the power, the tools, and the will to secure public security and order. As a democracy, it spread the power among the people; as a parliament, it wasted too much time in pointless deliberations; and as a republic, it lacked someone who could make the necessary decisions. These are all political flaws and they needed to be addressed politically. Because of the shortages of food just after the war and the rapid inflation during 1922 and 1923, Schmitt could have easily added complaints about economic instability. That he chose not to is a further indication of how little importance he attributed to economics. For Schmitt, the crucial issue was always the Hobbesian one of public security and order.

References

Bodin, Jean (2009)[1955] *On Sovereignty. Six Books of the Commonwealth.* Abridged and Translated by M.J. Tooley. Oxford: Seven Treasures Publications.

Schmitt, Carl (1923) "Soziologie des Souveränitätsbegriffes und politische Theologie." In *Hauptprobleme der Soziologie. Erinnerungsgabe für Max Weber.* Herausgegeben von Melchior Palyi. München und Leipzig: Verlag von Duncker und Humblot, II. Band. 3–36.

Schmitt, Carl (1964)[1921] *Die Diktatur. Von den Anfängen des modernen Souveränitätsgedanken bis zum proletarischen Klassenkampf.* Berlin: Duncker & Humblot. Dritte Auflage.

Schmitt, Carl (1982)[1921] *Politische Romantik.* Berlin: Duncler & Humblot. Vierte Auflage.

Schmitt, Carl (1996) *Die geistesgeschichtliche Lage des heutigen Parlamentarismus.* Berlin: Duncker & Humblot. Achte Auflage.

Schmitt, Carl (2002)[1923] *Römischer Katholizismus und politische Form.* Stuttgart: Klett-Cotta. Vierte Auflage.

Schmitt, Carl (2015)[1922] *Politische Theologie. Vier Kapitel zur Lehre von der Souveränität.* Berlin: Duncker & Humblot. Zehnte Auflage.

Schmitt, Carl (2016)[1912] *Gesetz und Urteil. Eine Untersuchung zum Problem der Rechtspraxis.* München: Verlag C.H. Beck.

Tönnies, Ferdinand (2019) *Ferdinand Tönnies Gesamtausgabe. Gemeinschaft und Gesellschaft 1880–1935.* Herausgegeben von Bettina Clausen und Dieter Haselbach. Berlin: Walter de Gruyter. 2019. Band 2.

4

Chaos Versus Dictator: 1924–1926

Abstract This chapter begins in 1924 and ends in 1926. The writings from these years are not as weighty as some of his earlier ones and they are not nearly as famous as some of his later ones. However, they are indicative of his growing reputation and of his increasing concern about the disorder in Germany. It is in these essays that he again attacks liberalism's emphasis on the individual and criticizes parliament because of its liberal leanings. And, it is here that Schmitt begins his examination of Article 48 of the Weimar constitution and his warning about the need for "public security and order."

Keywords Chaos • Dictator • Individual • Article 48 • Order

Compared to the years from 1914 until 1923, the period from the beginning of 1924 until the end of 1926 was a relatively calm one for Germany. Inflation had mostly subsided, street battles were rarer, and it seemed that the Weimar government was finally functioning. Thus, it appeared that Germany had finally settled into a somewhat stable period. The same thing seemed to apply to Carl Schmitt whose life was relatively stable in

© The Author(s) 2020

C. Adair-Toteff, *Carl Schmitt on Law and Liberalism*, Palgrave Studies in Classical Liberalism, https://doi.org/10.1007/978-3-030-57118-4_4

contrast to his earlier personal crises as well as to his academic setbacks of the previous decade. Now, as a professor of law at Bonn he was gaining the respect from some of his older colleagues and was attracting an increasing number of students. As a writer his reputation as both a provocative polemist and a thoughtful scholar continued to expand and his writings were being published in some of Germany's leading journals. And, even his private life seemed to have settled down to some extent. His marriage was mostly over but the fights with his wife had all but ceased. His life had markedly improved, both professionally and personally, and one might have thought that this would have made Schmitt slightly less anxious about the future. However, it did not; instead, he worried about the near future. He continued to caution about the Weimar constitution and to warn about the future. While others might have been lulled into thinking that the worse was over, he was under no such illusion. He felt compelled to issue warnings that Germany was confronted by internal and external enemies. Carl Schmitt did not regard himself as a modern-day Cassandra; rather, he was a modern version of the "apostle of fear."

The name Thomas Hobbes is conspicuously missing from most of the seven articles that Carl Schmitt published during the years 1924–1926, yet Hobbes' theme about the power of political fear permeates almost all of them. In Schmitt's writings during this period, it seems that disorder and even chaos were ready to break out at any moment, and in his considered opinion, only the dictator has the sufficient authority and the necessary powers to stop this outbreak—and then to begin to restore the public security and order. As with Hobbes, the notions of law and liberalism seem to recede into the background, yet their flaws and their failures remain present. These pieces appear almost incidental: they do not carry the punch of some of the earlier writings such as *Politische Theologie* and they are not nearly as famous as some of those of his later writings, like *Der Begriff des Politischen*. However, they provide a much clearer and a rather richer account of Schmitt's picture of the dictator's fight against disorder, and they pave the path toward his later "friend-foe" distinction as well as to his conception of who was the true defender of the Weimar constitution.

One of the Weimar constitution's staunchest defenders was Richard Thoma. Thoma was a defender not only of the constitution but of liberal democracy and as such he was often in conflict with Carl Schmitt. In 1925 Thoma published a review of Schmitt's *Die geistesgeschichtliche Lage des heutigen Parlamentarismus* in which he noted that it was both a pure scholarly analysis of some specific political ideas and an attempt at a composite of constitutional analysis and a prognosis for the future (Thoma 2008: 161–162). Thoma objected that Schmitt's declaration that parliamentarianism was dead was premature and he rejected Schmitt's call for a dictator. And, he complained that Schmitt's demand for combining the national dictator and the Catholic Church would fail in its attempt to restore order, discipline, and hierarchy (Thoma 2008: 165–167). Implicit in Thoma's critique was the objection that Schmitt violated Max Weber's cardinal rule not to conflate scholarly analysis and value judgments, a rule that Thoma scrupulously adhered to as evidenced by his contribution to the two-volume *Erinnerungsgabe für Max Weber*. Thoma's article was entitled "Der Begriff der modernen Demokratie in seinem Verhältnis zum Staatsbegriff. Prolegomena zu einer Analyse des demokratischen Staates der Gegenwart." Thoma's contribution followed Schmitt's article on sovereignty and differed in tone and in substance. In contrast to Schmitt's critical political essay, Thoma's article was a scholarly legal defense. In addition, Schmitt barely mentioned Weber whereas Thoma referenced Weber nine different times (Thoma 2008: 93, 101–102, 108, 114, and 119). Finally, there is the difference in approach: Schmitt's dogmatic approach is indicated by the book version's title: *Politische Theologie*. In contrast, Thoma offered a "Prolegomena" to an understanding of what democracy means for the present. Schmitt responded to Thoma in 1924 with a short, but highly critical, review. Like many of his attacks, this is a combination of analysis and value judgments. His analysis is focused mostly on the notion of modern democracy which Thoma differentiates into a "radical" type of democracy and a "liberal" one. The former is radical because it insists in an egalitarian ideal of freedom and the belief in equality for all. The latter is liberal because it is not egalitarian as it recognizes the natural inequality of human beings (Thoma 2008: 90–92; Schmitt 1988b: 19). Thoma also notes that while democracy is a "legal concept" ("Rechtsbegriff") it is more than a simple form of state because the modern incarnation of democracy is a representative one. Thus, modern democracy does not fit in the Aristotelian trinity of monarchy, aristocracy, and democracy (Thoma 2008: 98–100; Schmitt 1988b: 19). Thoma's second section is focused on the distinction between the juridical and the sociological conceptions of the state to which Schmitt agrees with Thoma's assertion that there is no sociological notion. And, Thoma chose not to answer the question of what a state is in itself (Thoma 2008: 106–107; Schmitt 1988b: 20). Thoma's third section on the relationship between the state and democracy is what interests Schmitt the most. Thoma's contention is that a state is a "collection of a people" ("Volksverband") and that it can be regarded as a "juridical person" ("juristischer Person"). As such a type of authority ("Herrschaft") it is less of a fiction than other forms of state. In addition, the more homogeneous the people are, the more it makes sense to talk about the "will of the people" ("Volkswille"). Schmitt concludes the analysis of Thoma's contribution by praising it as an "extraordinarily comprehensive treatise" ("außerordentlich reichhaltige Abhandlung") (Schmitt 1988b: 21). Yet, Schmitt faults Thoma for his reliance on everyday language because of its lack of conceptual clarity and he criticizes him for the lack of decisive answers to the question of who decides. It is as if Thoma had missed the most critical issue. However, Schmitt reserves his most aggressive criticism for Thoma's conception of the state as "people" ("Volk") and the idea that there can be a notion of the "will of the people" ("Volkswille") in a democracy. Schmitt concentrates on the issue of identity and points out that while it is rather difficult to determine a state's identity in a direct democracy, it is virtually impossible to do so in a representative democracy. This is even more problematic in a modern democracy where there are various political parties which offer competing claims to speak for the "people." Thus, there can be no real answer to the question of the "'true' will of the people" ("'wahre' Willen des Volkes") (Schmitt 1988b: 22–25).

In 1924 Schmitt returned again to the topic of dictator but it was in connection to Article 48 of the Weimar constitution. The title of this lengthy article indicates its historical focus with both the reference to the Presidents of the Reich and to Article 48: "Die Diktatur des Reichspräsidenten. nach Artikel 48 der Weimarer Verfassung." However much this article deals with specific historical facts, its main focus is on

Schmitt's recurring concern with the dangers to public security and order. The phrase "öffentliche Sicherheit und Ordnung" is found nine times throughout this article, including as a title of a subsection (Schmitt 1964b: 217, 224, 226, 227, 231, 232, and 245). The actual facts will be of interest to the historian; the concern here is on Schmitt's theory of the dictator and the implementation of military force to restore public security and order. Putting aside the historical points, Schmitt's article addresses four main points: one, what Article 48 says; two, what it means; three, what it does; and four, its implications.

As much as Article 48 seems to be clear and straightforward, Schmitt argues (convincingly) that it is not. He brings up a number of points which he believes are unclear, ambiguous, or simply wrong. One is the issue of what "public security and order" actually means. Is it a general reference or is it rather limited? Does it apply to all of Germany or to the specifically affected areas? Is this a practical matter or is it partially theoretical? Article 48 does not specifically address any of these issues. Another point is in reference to its "purpose" ("zu diesem Zwecke"): does this refer to the quelling of disorder or to the purpose of actually restoring order. If it is the latter, is it to return Germany to its previous state of order or to a heightened state of tranquility? If it is the latter, is this even possible? Finally, is Article 48 something that adds to the Reich president's power or does it limit it? These are questions regarding what Article 48 says; however, Schmitt's greater concern is with what Article 48 means.

Schmitt took issue with what he regarded as the general understanding of what Article 48 meant. He disagreed with the general interpretation that Article 48 was clear in what it meant and the general acceptance that it was intended as a limitation on the Reich president's powers (Schmitt 1964b: 218). He looks specifically at the seven fundamental rights that can be set aside during the time of disorder. These were Article 114 on personal freedom, Article 115 on living quarters, Article 117 on mail privacy, Article 118 on freedom of the press, Article 122 on freedom of association, and Article 124 on voter freedom (Weimarer Verfassung 1919: 8). This does not appear to be a limitation on the Reich president's powers but an extension of them. In addition, Schmitt directs attention to Article 105 in which the question of extraordinary tribunals is addressed. There, any type of "state of emergency" ("Ausnahmezustand") court is eliminated, along with military tribunals; the constitution makes it clear that only regular courts have legal validity (Weimarer Verfassung 1919: 17). While it may seem that Article 105 is not a very relevant issue today, it was crucial then because the Weimar constitution was adopted less than a year after the First World War had ended. Furthermore, this Article was important to Schmitt in light of some of his writings from the war.

Schmitt argued that the problems with the received interpretation of Article 48 run much deeper than already indicated. He indicates that at least two difficulties affect this Article. First is the problem of the seven fundamental rights. How can the constitution maintain that these seven rights belong to the most fundamental rights which are guaranteed to every German citizen and then allow these same fundamental rights to be revoked? Furthermore (and an anticipation of the later conflict between the German national government and the Prussia regional one), Schmitt points to the possible conflict between the Reich and the states ("Länder") (Schmitt 1964b: 220–221). The answer to both of these issues is a matter of decisionist power: there needs to be a supreme authority with the power to restore public security and order. This is what the Weimar constitution should be giving the "Reichs*exekutive*." Schmitt believed that he had mounted a rather compelling criticism against the popular reading of Article 48 so he focused his attention to the delineation of what he thought that particular article actually does (Schmitt 1964b: 224).

In order to explain what Article 48 is intended to accomplish, Schmitt considers several related points. One is what is meant when the Weimar constitution indicates that certain fundamental rights can be suspended ("außer Kraft setzen") or that the constitution can be set aside ("beseitigen"). Schmitt does not directly answer these issues; instead, he points to the fact that Paragraph 1 concerns life and death, whereas Paragraph 2 seems to deal with far less critical matters. His point is that there can be no real conflict between the two because the more critical issue (Paragraph 1) supersedes the less critical issue (Paragraph 2). Second, the preceding point seems to imply that one can suspend the lesser rights in order to safeguard the more important one; yet, Schmitt suggests that a closer and more detailed assessment of "außer Kraft" is warranted (Schmitt 1964b: 227–228). Schmitt recognized the importance of this phrase in part because it is used in both Paragraph 3 and Paragraph 4 of Article 48 (Weimarer Verfassung 1919: 8). Furthermore, he noted that the parliament recognized how much power this article gave the political leader—they regarded it as unusual and limitless and that they would have to rely on the political leader's sense of responsibility not to misuse it (Schmitt 1964b: 233).

Schmitt moved to take up the issue of what constitutes a national emergency and he explained that there are varying types of state emergencies. Some might require the implementation of rather minor restrictions and rules while others may require some more drastic measures. It is evident that Schmitt has little interest in minor problems and their remedies; instead, he focuses on major emergencies and the radical measures needed to deal with them. That is why he moved almost immediately to address the difference between a monarch and a sovereign dictator. A monarch rules during normal times and under normal circumstances; in contrast, the sovereign dictator must rule during abnormal times and under abnormal circumstances. In the past, a monarch did have considerable power, but even then, he often had to consult with advisors about the possible limits to his actions. But the modern king must contend with a constitution or something equally limiting. In both cases, the monarch exercised his power during normal conditions in contrast to the sovereign dictator who must act during a national crisis. Thus, a monarch may be sovereign but is not a dictator, but when the situation requires that the constitution can no longer be enforced, then the dictator must become sovereign (Schmitt 1964b: 234–238). While most commentators had focused on the first two paragraphs of Article 48, Schmitt's concern here was more with Paragraph 5. That has to do with how long the measures indicated in Paragraphs 1 and 2 can remain in effect; that is, how long can the political leader make use of the extreme measures given to him in accordance with the first two paragraphs of Article 48? The question is whether this power can be employed for an indeterminable or "unforeseeable time" ("unabsehbare Zeit") (Schmitt 1964b: 238–242). He suggests that the answer to this question can be found in the Paragraph 2 of Article 48. He reminds his readers that the constitution applies during normal times; hence, it is concerned with "normal order" ("normale Ordnung"). However, Paragraph 2 presupposes an "abnormal situation" ("abnorme Situation"), thus requires abnormal measures (Schmitt 1964b: 243–244). In other words, it lies outside the legal realm—even the Reichspräsident cannot offer a legal judgment because it is not a legal measure (Schmitt 1964b: 250–251). And, that means that legal regulations cannot apply to states of emergency because, as is frequently noted, extraordinary situations demand extraordinary means. It is not up to the normal state to determine how long the extraordinary measures need to be in place; it is solely the decision of the sovereign dictator (Schmitt 254–256). Furthermore, Schmitt explained that the extraordinary power that Article 48 confers is the main reason why there is such a range of opinions regarding it. And, that is why Schmitt concluded by reminding everyone that Article 48 was adopted during the abnormal situation of late summer 1919 and that the current situation is also abnormal. The times are not simple, so no simple answer can be given to the question how long can the extraordinary measures of Article 48 remain in effect (Schmitt 1964b: 258–259).

The following year Schmitt published "Das Ausführungsgesetz zu Art. 48 der Reichsverfassung (sog. Diktaturgesetz)." He repeated the dictum that extraordinary situations call for extraordinary measures and he insisted that the need to establish "public security and order" ("öffentliche Sicherheit und Ordung") meant that extraordinary means were needed. He insisted that such conditions meant that normal legal means would not be sufficient and that Article 48 served as the basis for such extrajudicial justification (Schmitt 1995d: 38–40). Instead there needs to be sufficient "leeway" ("Spielraum") in order to tackle such difficult problems and this might include house searches, temporary imprisonments, and confiscation of newspapers. It may also include the restriction of fundamental freedoms such as freedom of the press and freedom of association. And, it might require the sharpening of criminal penalties. Finally, it means that the length of time for the employment of these extraordinary measures may need to be extended. The person who decides these questions may be regarded as a dictator. However, Schmitt suggested that it is not a dictator who decides these questions; it is the Reichspräsident. And he reminds his readers that Article 48 was instituted during extraordinary times and that the current state is also extraordinary, thus requiring extraordinary measures (Schmitt 1995d: 41).

In 1925 Schmitt published a short article on the Reichspräsident and the Weimar constitution and anyone thinking that it would have little to do with his notion of a dictator would be dissuaded of that by its opening paragraph. In "Reichspräsident und Weimarer Verfassung" Schmitt noted that votes choose one single individual as president and that they place their trust in him. As a result, Schmitt downplays the importance of political parties and minimizes their influence. Instead, voters choose one man who will hold both legal and political power for the seven-year term and they will trust him to do what is right during normal as well as abnormal times. He may be a typical president during most of the time but he can become a dictator during a state of emergency. While this may seem dangerous, Schmitt points out that party prestige and even the Weimar constitution are really dangerous because of their artificiality (Schmitt 1995b: 24–25). He warned that an open conflict between the Reichspräsident and the parliament would be a catastrophe and that is why the voters give him more authority than they do to the legislators. To Schmitt, this is not merely an exercise in voting power, it is the opportunity to fundamentally change the way in which the Reichspräsident is able to act. The death of Reichspräsident Friedrich Ebert is to be mourned but he had personally put his own substantial mark on the presidency. Hence, Ebert would have also welcomed the possibility to change the status quo. Therefore, Schmitt insists that rather than considering Ebert's death as a tragedy, it should be regarded as an opportunity to be used to improve Germany's status. He concludes with the observation that Clemenceau had remarked that the French always choose the most stupid to be president and that the Germans must now choose the smartest one (Schmitt 1995b: 27).

The following year Schmitt published a book review. Neither the journal in which it was published nor the book itself was typical. The journal was the *Archiv für Sozialwissenschaft und Sozialpolitik* which had been reoriented in 1904 under the new editorship of Edgar Jaffé, Werner Sombart, and Max Weber. By 1926 they had made the *Archiv* into the leading socio-political journal, and while two of the editors had resigned and Weber had died, the journal continued to be one of the most highly regarded journals in Germany. And the book, *Die Idee der Staatsräison in der neueren Geschichte*, was written by the highly respected Berlin professor and political thinker Friedrich Meinecke. It was one thing to argue with Richard Thoma about parliament and constitutional issues because Thoma was "just" a legal scholar and the issues were relatively minor. But it was another thing to address one of the most famous German thinkers and on the issue of the nation state in modern history. Schmitt began his review with an acknowledgment of Meinecke's considerable importance and the significant relevance of his book. He acknowledged Meinecke's mastery of the topic and praised his immense knowledge of the past 400 years of political thinking. But he hinted at the inherent difficulty in locating the real answer to the question for the existence of the state hidden in the "mosaic of the thousand nuances" ("Mosaik der tausend Nuancen"). One minute it is Machiavellianism, another it is power politics, and another it is the "life-will of the states" ("Lebenswille der Staaten") (Schmitt 1988c: 45). This multiplicity of views is matched by the book's lack of conceptual clarity and its lack of structure. What takes its place is a number of dualisms, which range from the contrast between being ("Sein") and should ("Sollen"), between power ("Macht") and morality ("Sittlichkeit"). While Meinecke notes the oppositions, his sympathies appear to be on the side of the ethical, the good, the reasonable, and the rational. Yet, history reveals that that is rarely the case. In fact, Schmitt argued that because Meinecke was such an excellent German historian, he ended up dwelling on the progressive period of Friedrich the Great. And, that meant that Meinecke was unable to recognize how abnormal the current state of affairs was, but it also meant that his account of absolutism was distorted (Schmitt 1988c: 47–52).

Meinecke's failure to provide a correct account of absolutism prompted Schmitt to write his own. It was a brief article but he made a number of important corrections to Meinecke's book. The term absolutism is a relatively modern term and Schmitt noted that its usage began around 1600. It referred to an absolute monarch who regarded the state as his own; this sentiment was expressed best in the claim "L'État c'est moi." This monarch possessed absolute power and he used it to fulfill his will. His soldiers, his authorities, and even his subjects had one single purpose which was to serve the king. While Schmitt conceded that prior to 1600 many kings had considerable power but he countered that with the claim that those kings were more than rivaled by the authority and power of the

Roman Catholic Church. It was only with the Reformation that the Church began to lose its power and provided the monarch to become absolute. Without naming either Meinecke or Friedrich the Great, Schmitt suggested that the best instance of an absolute monarch is one in which the king is enlightened and has trained bureaucrats who will eagerly and fairly carry out his progressive decrees (Schmitt 1995c: 95). And, while Schmitt did not name Hobbes, his description of the absolute state construed as a purposeful, functioning machine is certainly similar to Hobbes' concept of the state. This is also supported by Schmitt's emphasis on reason. However, he also indicates the importance of Machiavelli and Bodin for the notion of sovereignty.

Schmitt turned his attention to the growing opposition to absolutism and how its detractors regarded absolutism as a form of tyranny. Despots were not to be feared and obeyed; rather people should have repudiated them and to have rebelled against them. The first group that Schmitt discussed were those who believed that they had the fundamental right to kill the tyrant—these were the "monarchomachen." The second group was composed of the English and French thinkers who justified revolution—Locke and Montesquieu who objected to the concentration of power in the hands of just one man. Instead, they believed that power should be divided. Rather than a single figure in a central state, these thinkers believed that power should be shared with parliament, thereby ensuring freedom. The third group objected to the concept of the state as a machine and argued that it was not a functioning mechanism but was a living organism. The supporters of this theory tended to be Romantics (Schmitt 1995c: 96–97).

Schmitt noted that no sovereign is absolute and no monarch has absolute power. They must contend with other powerful institutions such as churches and courts. Rather than simply being a matter of power, it is also an issue of good and evil. Schmitt indicated that the conception of the monarch as determining questions of morality was promoted by Hobbes, but he was influenced by his religious convictions. He suggested that the classical notion of the state as determining what is right and wrong was Rousseau's conception of the state embodying the will of the people. However, this is no longer a matter of absolutism but is an issue of freedom, which leads to Schmitt's discussion of the struggle between Church and State.

The liberalism of the nineteenth century suggested that freedom for the individual was the highest good, and liberals insisted that the Church needed to leave matters of marriage, family, and education to non-religious entities. There were not many real liberals in Germany during the second half of the nineteenth century and certainly Bismarck was not one of them. However, he did believe that the Church should not be the highest authority; instead, it should be the state. This conviction led to the German "Kulturkampf" in the 1870s between Bismarck's government and the Catholic Church. However, the German emphasis on the importance of the state is found much earlier. Schmitt singles out Hegel's political philosophy as the key influence and while it gave rise to the modern rational state it also served as the foundation for radical socialism (Schmitt 1995c: 98–99). Schmitt concludes by offering a defense of absolutism but not simply for the state. Modern political theories from both the Right and the Left had forgotten the fact that the state was originally regarded as having divine origins and was a necessary consequence of the social nature of humans. While it is important to give to the state that which is due to it, Schmitt reminds us that it is equally, if not more, important to give to God what rightfully belongs to him. And, Schmitt also reminds us that while we must obey men, it is more important to obey God (Schmitt 1995c: 99).

Finally, Schmitt published an entry on the dictator in the "Staatslexikon" of the "Görres-Gesellschaft." Founded in the 1870s it was an association committed to scholarship and science but with a Catholic approach. As such, its "Staatslexikon" was an ideal forum for Schmitt to offer a brief account of the meaning and history of the notion of the dictator. He traced its beginnings to the Romans, moved through the Renaissance, to the French Revolution, and finally to the Bolshevik one. But his main interest was not historical but contemporary so he differentiated between the "commissary dictatorship" and the "sovereign dictatorship"—the former works within the legal framework while the latter must act extrajudicially. The former is linked to a political party and is somewhat restricted by its policies while the latter has full authority to restore "public security and order" ("öff.[entliche] Sicherheit und Ordnung") (Schmitt 1995e:

35). Again, the individual who has the power to do so is the Reichspräsident and has the extraordinary authority to do so because of the extraordinariness of the situation. It is clarifying to read Schmitt's opening sentence which is his definition of the dictator: "Dictatorship is the practice of being freed from the legal limitation on state force for the purpose of overcoming an abnormal situation, in particular war and rebellion" ("Diktatur ist die Ausübung einer von rechtl.[liche] Schranken befreiten staatl.[lichen] Gewalt zum Zweck der Überwindung eines abnormen Zustands, inbes.[sonderes] Krieg und Aufruhr") (Schmitt 1995e: 33). For the genuine dictator, there cannot be any legitimate constraints on his authority and his power—he has one and only one purpose and that is to restore "public security and order." He has the means and is entitled to use them until he determines that safety and order have been restored and that the state has returned to normal. Schmitt's preoccupation with the concept of the dictator began before this three-year period and it would last past it: *Diktatur* was published in 1921 and Schmitt would put out the second edition in 1928. And, by 1924, the time of enormous inflation had mostly passed and it seemed that there was a sense of normalcy in Germany. However, Carl Schmitt suspected that this sense of peace was only temporary and he was warning of future unrest. Thomas Hobbes may have been in the back of Schmitt's mind because he was following the cautions of the "apostle of fear."

References

Schmitt, Carl (1988a) *Positionen und Begriffe. Im Kampf mit Weimar-Genf-Versailles 1923–1939*). (1940). Berlin: Duncker & Humblot.

Schmitt, Carl (1988b) "Der Begriff der modernen Demokratie in seinem Verhältnis zum Staatsbegriff." (1924). In Schmitt 1988a. 19–25.

Schmitt, Carl (1988c) "Zu Friedrich Meineckes 'Idee der Staatsräson." In Schmitt 1988a. 45–51.

Schmitt, Carl (1964a) *Die Diktatur. Vom den Anfängen des modernen Souveränitätsgedanken bis zum proletarischen Klassenkampf.* Berlin: Duncker & Humblot.

Schmitt, Carl (1964b) "Die Diktatur des Reichspräsidenten nach Artikel 48 der Weimarer Verfassung." In Schmitt 1964a. 215–261.
Schmitt, Carl (1995a) *Staat, Großraum, Nomos. Arbeiten aus den Jahren 1916–1969.* Herausgegeben, mit einem Vorwort und mit Anmerkungen versehen von Günter Maschke. Berlin: Duncker & Humblot.
Schmitt, Carl (1995b) "Reichspräsident und Weimarer Verfassung." In Schmitt 1995a. 24–32.
Schmitt, Carl (1995c) "Absolutismus." In Schmitt 1995a. 95–101.
Schmitt, Carl (1995d) "Das Ausführungsgesetz zu Art. 49 der Reichsverfassung (sog. Diktaturgesetz)." In Schmitt 1995a. 38–43.
Schmitt, Carl (1995e) "Diktatur." In Schmitt 1995a. 33–37.
Thoma, Richard (2008) *Rechtstaat-Demokratie-Grundrechte. Ausgewählte Abhandlungen aus fünf Jahreszehnten.* Herausgegeben und eingeleitet von Horst Dreier. Tübingen: Mohr Siebeck.
Weimarer Verfassung (1919) *Die Weimarer Verfassung.*

5

Politics or Law: 1927–1928

Abstract This chapter focuses on the years 1927 and part of 1928 and it reveals the tension in Schmitt's thinking regarding the relationship between law and politics. The writings from these years contain some further criticisms of parliament and democracy. The problem with the former is that it is too often the forum for endless discussions and the problem with the latter is the claim of pluralism. What Germany needed was a single leader and one to represent the people's will.

Keywords Politics • Law • Pluralism • Parliament • State

The years 1927 and 1928 were rather good for Germany. Inflation had subsided, manufacturing was increasing, and Germany was being accepted again as a world power. This was signified by its treaty with Italy and even more so by its acceptance into the League of Nations. These years were also somewhat good for Carl Schmitt. His reputation as a legal scholar was growing, especially with the publication of his book on the Weimar constitution. But it was especially indicated by his call to a professorship in Berlin. During this time, he was preoccupied with the idea

© The Author(s) 2020

C. Adair-Toteff, *Carl Schmitt on Law and Liberalism*, Palgrave Studies in Classical Liberalism, https://doi.org/10.1007/978-3-030-57118-4_5

of law and particularly with the concept of the constitution. But he was also concerned with politics and he returned his focus to the opposition between parliament and modern democracy.

In 1926 Schmitt published an essay with the title that reflected that opposition: “Der Gegensatz von Parlamentarismus und moderner Massendemokratie.” In it, Schmitt referred to comments that he had made in his *Geistigesgeschichtliche Lage des heutigen Parliamentarismus* about the relevance and need for discussion and openness, as well as about modern mass democracy. But this essay was not a simple rehash of points he had made in that earlier book; instead, it includes a renewed attempt to spell out exactly what was wrong with contemporary liberalism. He contended that the classical representatives of political liberalism were convinced that not only was public discussion an antidote to corruption, but that it had moral value for parliamentary measures. They had insisted that parliament was the place for mounting arguments and counter arguments and that this process would help guarantee the truth and correctness of their political decisions. These, he held, made up the “spiritual foundation” (“geistige Grundlage”) of parliament and that the major features of it were discussion and openness (Schmitt 1988b: 52–53).

Since 1923 the belief in the great virtues of discussion and openness had grown old, so Schmitt thought it was time to reconsider the connection between parliament and democracy. As he had done in his earlier book, Schmitt objected to the historical association of the one with the other and the inability, or the unwillingness, to recognize that they were not the same. Instead, Schmitt insisted that there is a need to admit that there may be a better form of institution than the parliament to confront the communism from the Left and the dictatorship from the Right. But it is also important to recognize the belief that the representative is independent of the voter and the party, just as it is crucial to note that the representative has the freedom to speak openly. A further claim was that parliament provided the best platform to minimize political amateurism and that it offered the most reliable place to select the best political leader (Schmitt 1988b: 54–55). Schmitt not only objected to any contemporary claim but countered that historically it was also false. He drew attention to the fact that during the past century, the numerous parliaments have mostly failed to choose the best educated and the most responsible leaders, not to mention that they have also failed to elect the best political "Führer."

Although this belief in parliament is English in origin and is portrayed as practical, it is still nothing more than an ideal. Similarly, public discussions are ostensibly aimed at determining the best choice, but it is also not much more than an ideal. It is an ideal because it presupposes that the exchange of ideas is honest and that the opponent can be won over by rational arguments which are based on truth and correctness. It presupposes that the people debating are doing so independent of party politics and free from any self-interest. However, Schmitt reminded his readers that almost no one believes those presuppositions are applicable today. His conclusion is that this skepticism is why there is so little trust in the German Parliament (Schmitt 1988b: 56). Instead, the traditional belief in parliament is nothing more than empty formalism and the belief in the efficacy of public discussion has been replaced by the conviction that this is nothing more than superficial decorations. In fact, what is currently believed is that there is no such thing as a difference of opinion; rather, it is an opposition between different social and economic groups. And, there is no possibility for genuine compromise and coalition; there is only the appeal to special interest and particular power (Schmitt 1988b: 57). Schmitt asks, who today believes that ideas meet in parliament, their movement strikes a spark, and leads to evidence? And, he questions Bentham's claim that public openness matters as well as asking who still thinks of parliament as the "great 'Tribunal'" ("große 'Tribune'")? When Max Weber, Hugo Preuß, and Friedrich Naumann had spoken and written about the promise of parliament, they believed that. But no one today would believe in those hopes (Schmitt 1988b: 55, 58). The idea of parliament has gone, just as the period of the monarchy has passed. In light of this, Schmitt insisted that it is time to re-examine the concept of democracy.

Schmitt began his section on democracy by pointing out that while those who believe in parliament, believe in a government that is directed by discussion, which is a major tenet of liberalism. However, that belief in government by discussion does not belong to democracy and that democracy and parliament are not the same. He adds that that is especially true in regard to modern mass democracy. Democracy does not adhere to the belief in multiple points of view; modern mass democracy believes in equality. That not only means that there must be a homogeneous group; it necessarily means the rejection, if not elimination, of the heterogeneous. Schmitt offers two illustrations: one is the radical emigration of Greeks in Turkey and the other is the laws against immigration in Australia. He takes it as a matter of political power for a democracy to stop the "foreign and unequal" ("Fremde und Ungleiche") from threatening the homogeneity (Schmitt 1988b: 59). While this has been historically true, it is even more so today. But Schmitt clarifies that political homogeneity does not necessitate economic equality. Nor does it mean that a colonial power must be equal to its colony; in fact, just as the upper class is above the lower class, so does the imperial power rule the colony. And, while England may believe in equality and voter rights, it does not grant them to all. In the same way, ancient Athens regarded itself as a paradigm of democracy, but did not permit slaves to vote. It is laudable in principle to say that all are equal, but it is honest to admit that that is not the case. Great Britain is a commonwealth and a world power but it does not allow all its "citizens" to participate in voting. And, Schmitt insists that much the same can be said about France and other powers. Thus, the belief in equality and homogeneity in modern mass democracy is an illusion. However, the belief in the equality of all people is not a matter for democracy; it is the conviction of modern liberalism. And, this belief in equality stems from the belief that the modern state is based upon a mutual contract—a belief that began with Rousseau and his contention that there is a "volonté Générale" (Schmitt 1988b: 61–63).

The modern parliament may believe that it is threaten from the Left by the Bolsheviks and from the Right by the Fascists, but in reality, it is threatened by three crises: the crisis of democracy, the crisis of the modern state, and the crisis of parliament. But it is an error to think that communism and fascism are necessarily anti-democratic. Like every dictatorship, both are anti-liberal, but throughout history, dictators have often been democratic. And, they have often spoken through the "will of the people." Schmitt insisted that the notion of a "people" ("Volk") is a concept of public law and that it exists only in the public. Furthermore, he maintained that the single opinion of a hundred million private people is neither the "will of the people" nor "public opinion" ("öffentliche

Meinung") (Schmitt 1988b: 64–65). To think otherwise is an illusion; just as the belief that if communism and fascism can be kept at a distance then the contemporary crisis of parliamentarianism will be solved. However, it can be solved only when the link between parliamentarianism and democracy is finally severed. And, that means overcoming the link between the liberalism's individualism and the turn to a genuine conception of democratic homogeneity (Schmitt 1988b: 65–66).

Carl Schmitt's *Der Begriff des Politischen* is his most famous work, and when it was published in 1932, it drew considerable attention—some positive but a fair amount was negative. However, Schmitt had first written it as a short essay and it appeared in the *Archiv für Sozialwissenschaft und Sozialpolitik* in 1927. That book will be explored in a later chapter; here the focus is on the article. But first, a point of clarification: Schmitt wrote about the contrast between "Gesellschaft" ("society") and "Gemeinschaft" ("community") and this contrast would have been familiar to many of the readers of the *Archiv für Sozialwissenschaft und Sozialpolitik* because it was a contrast that Schmitt had borrowed from Ferdinand Tönnies. Tönnies had first published his most important book *Gemeinschaft und Gesellschaft* in 1887. A second edition followed in 1912, and by 1920 it had gone from being a neglected work to being a classic. Between 1920 and 1926, it went through a number of editions and it appeared in an eighth edition in 1935, a year before Tönnies died.

In *Gemeinschaft und Gesellschaft*, Tönnies distinguished between two fundamentally different social groups. Put simply, the "Gemeinschaft" was a rural, agricultural, and family oriented group of people. It was traditional, small, and cohesive. It was based primarily on what Tönnies referred to as "Wesenwille," that is, "essential will" which embodied careful thinking. Again, put simply, "Gesellschaft" was a modern, urban, and unrelated collection of individuals. This collection was resistant to tradition, large, and atomistic. It embodied what Tönnies called "Kurwille" or "arbitrary will" (Tönnies 1991). If the "Gemeinschaft" was predicated on warmth and property, "Gesellschaft" was based upon cold calculation and money. The main point to keep in mind when reading Schmitt's "Der Begriff des Politischen" is Tönnies' depiction of "Gemeinschaft" as a unity ("Einheit") in contrast to "Gesellschaft" as a plurality. The former indicates coherence; the latter reveals multiplicity. For Tönnies, this was a matter of contrasting the unity of the past with the multiplicity of the future; it was wistfully reflective on how things once were. For Schmitt, this was a matter of contrasting the multiplicity of the present with the unity of the future. This was no instance for wishful thinking; it was a matter of immediate urgency. But one does not notice that call for action because it is hidden under the mantel of a thoughtful piece. Unlike the shocking opening sentence of *Politische Theologie,* the first sentences of "Der Begriff des Politischen" are mundane—Schmitt notes that observers who consider the economic struggle of the workers will recognize that their most powerful weapon is the strike. It is the workers' way to confront the injuries and injustices that the factory owners and the bosses inflict upon them and to cause difficulties in meeting production quotas and deadlines. And, many observers have concluded that the state is powerless against the power of the strike. They cannot intervene on behalf of the capitalists and this inability suggests an even greater defect. In fact, some thinkers have even predicted the death of the state along with any notion of sovereignty. Schmitt argues that one scholar who denied the sovereignty of the state and who insisted on pluralism was Harold Laski. According to Schmitt, Laski held that the individual was a member of many different associations, including a church, a union, a sporting club, among others. Thus, Laski held that there could be no unity but only pluralism (Schmitt 1988c: 67). Laski held up Bismarck's "Kulturkampf" as an example of a government that revealed that it was not all powerful but rather weak and that it was just the "superficial manner of speaking of jurists" who claimed that the state was all powerful. But for Schmitt this is really a matter of "friend" ("Freund") and "foe" ("Feind") and he added that neither the Roman Catholic Church nor any union had proclaimed a war against the state. Nor could Bismarck officially proclaim a war against the Church because he lacked the legal grounds ("jus belli") to do so. But if he had decided to announce who the enemy was, then he could have had legal sovereignty and political unity. Because political unity is essentially a definitive unity, regardless of whether this is a physical power or not, it is still the highest and most decisive level of unity. The problem with Laski's pluralism is that he lacks a coherent and definitive notion of politics. His social liberalism means that he sees everything as simply associations; hence, he cannot reach a clear definition of the political. As such, his belief in pluralism blinds him to the importance of the "Freund-Feind" distinction.

Schmitt contended that the state, which is essentially a political unity, has the fundamental right to the "jus belli," which he defined as the real possibility to name the enemy and to fight him. In Schmitt's account, it does not really matter which means the state chooses in this struggle; what matters is that the enemy is identified and the fight begins (Schmitt 1988c: 69). He quotes Emil Lederer's words from an earlier article in the *Archiv für Sozialwissenschaft und Sozialpolitik*: "Wir können sagen, daß sich am Tage der Mobilisierung die Gesellschaft, die bis dahin bestand, in eine Gemeinschaft umformte" ("We could say that on the day of the mobilization, what had been up to then was transformed from society into community"). Lederer was not just the author of this 1915 article; he was also one of the editors of the *Archiv* (Schmitt 1988c: 69, and footnote 1). As such, this was no minor comment but one which carried considerable weight because it not only spoke for all Germans but it represented the view of one of the most widely respected German thinkers. For Schmitt, the idea of the state of war was the most powerful concentration of strength that a state could have. The definitive political unity of the state meant that its population was ready to die for it as well as ready to kill for it, and that meant that the state more or less had the power to determine the life or death of its citizens. Schmitt admitted that there have been those who chose martyrdom for the church and there have been those who have even sacrificed their lives for economic conditions. However, he insisted that the religious martyrs sacrificed their physical lives for the sake of their individual souls and not the organization. In the same way, those who died for economics did so for themselves and not for the union and certainly not for the factory owner. As Schmitt put it bluntly, "[t]o earnestly demand that men should kill and be ready to die in order that trade and industry of the survivors can bloom or that the power of consumption of the grand children can expand is gruesome and insane."[1] Schmitt regards those who shirk their responsibility to the state

[1] "Von den Menschen im Ernst zu fordern, daß sie Menschen töten und bereit sind, zu sterben, damit Handel und Industrie der Überlebenden blühe oder die Komsumkraft der Enkel gedeihe, ist grauenhaft und verrückt" (Schmitt 1988c: 70).

as cowardly and those who naïvely proclaim "never again war" ("nie wieder Krieg") as circulating "manifest deception" ("manifester Betrug") (Schmitt 1988c: 71). Schmitt insisted that in war, the readiness of men to kill those on the enemy side is not an issue of norms, but is a genuine matter of existence. He also maintained that war cannot be grounded on ethics or norms and there can be no attempt to legitimize it or to justify it. Since Grotius, the notion of justice does not belong to the concept of war. Instead, it is really a matter of existence—either we live and the enemy dies or they live and we die. Schmitt maintained that the real essence of political existence resides in the unified determination between "Freund/Feind" and the decision to go to war. A state that lacks that determination and fails to decide is no longer a state. He repeats that the decision to go to war cannot be based either upon some high ideal or upon some legal norm; it can only make sense if it is founded on the realization that there is an enemy which is a genuine threat (Schmitt 1988c: 71). Schmitt argued that all of the people ("Volk") need to be united in believing that there is an enemy and that this is a political decision and not a personal one. In addition, it is misguided to think that simply by announcing that everyone is a friend does not make it so. Instead, the state needs to take up its authority and to recognize its need to be the "[p]rotection against external foes" ("Schutz gegen äußere Feinde"). And, he emphasizes the "eternal connection" ("ewiger Zusammenhang") between protection and obedience. This is why Schmitt explicitly invokes Hobbes' remark in *Leviathan* that there is a "mutual relation between Protection and Obedience." At the conclusion, Hobbes wrote, "And thus I have brought to an end my Discourse of Civil and Ecclesiastical Government, occasioned by the disorders of the present time, without partiality, without application, and without other designe, than to set before mens eyes the mutuall Relation between Protection and Obedience, of which the condition of Humane Nature and the Laws Divine, (both Naturall and Positive) require inviolable observation" (Hobbes 2005: 567). This comment by Hobbes is crucial for Schmitt for a number of reasons: first, it reveals the importance of Hobbes' political philosophy for him; and second, it bolsters Schmitt's claim that the primary function of the state is to protect its citizens from enemies; and third, it underscores his belief that there needs to be reciprocation between the state and its citizens. The state protects the citizens and the citizens obey the state. Following Hobbes, Schmitt contends that they are mutually necessary and that one has to accompany the other (Schmitt 1988c: 72).

Schmitt returned to his criticism of Laski and pluralism. Schmitt admitted that not every state was a unity but he questioned whether they could even be regarded as a state since it could not identify its enemy, much less protect its citizens. And, he suggested that these countries could naturally have an economy, morals, law, and art, but they would lack politics and could not be a state. Furthermore, he cautioned against the idyllic thought that an end of a world war would lead to world peace. Instead, he appealed to human nature that "humanity" ("Menschheit") is not a political concept but that when a state claims to be engaged in a war in the name of humanity, it is attempting to disguise the fact that it is really only a single state that is engaged in fighting another state—an enemy state. Thus, there is no humanity involved, only states. In a similar vein, Schmitt argued that the claim that there is an international organization is a misnomer because it is really about several states. Schmitt concluded by warning against pluralism and the belief that social grouping can somehow lead to peace. If a "world state" ("Weltstaat") ever came into being (which in Schmitt's view is an impossibility), it would mean the elimination of any political unity as well as the destruction of any political character.

From this article, one can conclude that Schmitt valued safety above anything else and that he was convinced that there would always be conflicts so that the state was necessary. But rather than thinking that the state should be concerned with the welfare of its citizens, he believed that the state existed solely for protection. And, that the citizens owed the state obedience for its protection. While the distinction "Freund/Feind" became a crucial and famous notion for Schmitt's reputation, in this essay he was not concerned with friends but only with foes. And, law and liberalism were lacking in offering any type of safety against the enemy.

Carl Schmitt's *Volksentscheid und Volksbegehren (People's Decision and People's Desire)* may appear at first glance to be a narrowly focused legal work. After all, it began as an address to the "Juristischen Gesellschaft" in Berlin. However, the lengthy subtitle hints at something more with the inclusion of the phrase "immediate democracy." The subtitle reads: *Ein Beitrag zur Auslegung der Weimarer Verfassung und zur Lehre von der Unmittelbaren Demokratie (An Essay to Explain the Weimar Constitution and on the Doctrine of Immediate Democracy).* Schmitt objected to the conflation of the two terms: "Volksentscheidung" and "Volksbegehren" and argued that they are fundamentally different. "Volksentscheidung" is the people's *decision* and is basically a referendum on some decision. As such, it occurs after the fact and seeks to alter the decision or to affirm it. "Volksbegehren" is the people's *desire* so it is an indication of what the people want. As such, it occurs prior to any decision and is used in order to indicate what the people wish. Another name for it is "Volksinitiative" ("People's initiative") which also clarifies that it is an initiative that comes from the people as opposed to the people's response to the decision that has been determined by the government (Schmitt 2014: 8–12). Schmitt concludes this section by stressing how extraordinary and important the "Volksbegehren" is (Schmitt 2014: 20).

Much of the second section revolves around the decisions about Germany's budget; however, toward the end Schmitt notes that throughout Europe there has been a concerted effort to reduce the opportunities for the people to be able to put forth initiatives. Instead, the authorities were demanding that the people should be even more trusting of their decisions. This is particularly troubling when it revolves around issues of taxes and expenditures. How can the people have any say in either how and how much the state takes in or how the state decides what to pay for and to whom? Schmitt insisted that this not only diminished the impact that the people might have on future decisions but also covered up the mistakes that the government makes as well as hides the members' corruption (Schmitt 2014: 37. 43–47).

The third and final section is the most relevant because it deals with the issue of what a "Volk" is and how it is related to the limits of immediate democracy. It is also the one that Schmitt expanded upon from his original Berlin speech. As he had suggested in the first section, "Volk" is open to many interpretations and these are relevant when one is referring to the people with respect to referendums and initiatives (Schmitt 2014: 14). Non-Germans may find it difficult to comprehend how crucial the term "Volk" is for Germans. Article 1 of the Weimarer Verfassung contains two sentences: "Das Reich ist eine Republik. Die Staatsgewalt geht vom Volke aus" ("The Reich is a republic. The power of the state is derived from the Volk") (Weimarer Verfassung. Artikel 1). Schmitt insisted that the question about laws regulating money help illuminate the limits to immediate democracy. Before explaining this, Schmitt noted that too often there is the belief that democracy equals the "Volk" but that is not only superficial but also somewhat misleading. And, he insists that his use of the term "Volk" is derived from the nature of the matter, from the method of determining the "Volkswillen" ("People's wills"), and from the "ideal and moral" principles of democracy (Schmitt 2014: 48). It is one thing for the Weimar constitution to insist on the crucial importance of the "Volk," but it is another thing to attempt to discern what it actually means. Schmitt argued that it does not signify one thing, but has a variety of meanings. And, these meanings occur in various forms: legal, political, and sociological. In the Weimar constitution it actually has a narrow scope because it refers to those who vote. Schmitt's assertion may not seem accurate but he bases it on the notion that the "Volk" has constitutional power. Those who come to vote have the power; those who choose to remain at home do not (Schmitt 2014: 49–50). But he clarifies that this is applicable in terms of a people's decision; it does not apply to a people's initiative because those numbers tend to be far smaller than those who actually vote. Furthermore, he draws a contrast with those who indicate their support for the government by their voting to affirm, in contrast to those who are not in support of the government as indicated by their initiative which seeks to alter what the state has decided to do. Yet, both cases point to a problem about the "Volk" in a democracy—originally there was an opposition between the magistrate who ruled and the people who were ruled. For support, he cites both Theodor Mommsen's monumental book on Roman law and the Brother Grimm's classic dictionary (Schmitt 2014: 51 and note 40). In addition, Schmitt points to another problem about democracy. On the one hand, democracy implies the ability to assemble publicly to discuss the people's concerns. On the other hand, democracy insists on the use of the secret ballot. Thus, there is a crucial tension between public openness and transparency and private opinion and secrecy. Schmitt goes so far as to suggest that the secret ballot destroys the "specific possibilities of the assembled people" ("spezifische

Möglichkeiten des versammelten Volkes" (Schmitt 2014: 51). Furthermore, the secret ballot eliminates one of the most fundamental principles of leadership—the principle of acclamation. Rousseau had drawn attention to the importance of acclamation by insisting that the people need to be able to assemble in order to shout their acclamation for the leader or to vocally express their dissatisfaction. Schmitt lists the various ways in which a people have been able to express their opinions: with a loud shout or a low call, by jubilation or a murmur, with a wave of a sword or a smack on the shield, or with a simple "Amen." Schmitt's point is while the means may vary, acclamation is a vital and necessary part of politics. He insisted that "[t]he acclamation is an eternal phenomenon of every political community. No state without people, no people without acclamation" ("Die Akklamation ist ein ewiges Phänomen jeder politischen Gemeinschaft. Kein Staat ohne Volk. Kein Volk ohne Akklamation") (Schmitt 2014: 52). Thus, there is an opposition between modern mass democracies and classical immediate democracies. And, it is clear which one Schmitt favored—the classical democracy was "genuine" ("echte") and "pure" ("reine") and that the secret ballot was one given by the "isolated, non-responsible private individual" ("isolierten, unverantwortlichen Privatmann") (Schmitt 2014: 53). In contrast, those who assemble and give their acclamation are doing so jointly, responsibly, and openly. Liberalism relies on the individual, but that does not reflect the will of the people. By assembling and acclaiming the leader they show that they are "one" and that they follow the "Führer's" instinct for determining who is friend and who is foe (Schmitt 2014: 54). An additional drawback of the secret ballot is that the voter is given only two choices: yes or no, and that the voter is denied the opportunity to gain clarification or to demand more information. In contrast, with immediate democracy, the "Führer" will react to hints that his audience does not understand him and will correct and amend what he is saying in order to clarify his position (Schmitt 2014: 57). Schmitt then returns to the theme of his second section, the one on finance, and it is such a topic that does not allow the binary choice of a secret ballot. It is also one that demands that those who vote on it have an understanding. Most questions are difficult to formulate into an either/or question, but it is especially true regarding the complexity in matters of finance. People need to be educated in order to begin to comprehend; while they need not be experts, they do need some context and information in order to make an informed decision (Schmitt 2014: 62–63). That leads to the juxtaposition between ruler and ruled and he invokes Weber's definition of "political ruling of men over men" ("Regierung dagegen bedeutet politische Herrschaft von Menschen über Menschen") (Schmitt 2014: 67). So, the matter of the "Volksinitiative" lies in the relationship between magistrate and "Volk." This is especially true with respect to an initiative for a law because it is promoted by the "Volk" and not by either the magistrate nor by the administrators. And it is prompted by the specific political unity of the people and it may imply the elimination of the magistrate (Schmitt 2014: 71, 74–75).

Schmitt concluded by addressing the notion of a state which lacks a magistrate and he suggested that this is promoted by two groups. One is the anarchists who argue that referendum is actually a falsification of the will of the people, but in reality, it is prompted by their hatred of the idea of a magistrate. The other group is composed of English liberals who think the idea of a magistrate thwarts democratic progress (Schmitt 2014: 76–77). Regarding the latter group, Schmitt drew attention to its foundation upon Rousseau's idyllic conception of democracy, and to the former group, he pointed to the intersection of politics and finance in Marxism. In both cases, the matter of taxation is important. For the liberals, there is the traditional cry of "no taxation without representation" and for the Marxists it is a matter of who counts as the people. Who among the people is to be compelled to pay taxes is the question which has no easy answer. And, that is partially because of the multiple meanings of the concept "Volk."

During 1927 and 1928, it appears that Schmitt was remaining ambivalent about politics and law. Sometimes he seemed to favor politics and attempted to reduce everything to the political—as in his "Freund-Feind" opposition. Other times he seems to side with law—but never uncritically. The next several years would continue to show the tension between law and politics, but it also reveals why he was consistently regarded as one of the finest constitutional scholars during the years of the Weimar government.

References

Hobbes, Thomas (2005) *Leviathan*. A Critical Edition by G.A.J. Rogers and Karl Schumann. London: Continuum International Publishing Group. Vol. 2.

Schmitt, Carl (1988a) *Positionen und Begriffe. Im Kampf mit Weimar-Genf-Versailles 1923–1939*. Berlin: Duncker & Humblot.

Schmitt, Carl (1988b) "Der Gegensatz von Parlamentarismus und moderner Massendemokratie." In Schmitt 1988a. 52–66.

Schmitt, Carl (1988c) "Der Begriff des Politischen." In Schmitt 1988a. 67–75.

Schmitt, Carl (2014) *Volksentscheid und Volksbegehren. Ein Beitrag zur Auslegung der Weimarer Verfassung und Zur Lehre von unmittelbaren Demokratie*. Berlin: Duncker & Humblot.

Tönnies, Ferdinand (1991) *Gemeinschaft und Gesellschaft. Grundbegriffe der reinen Soziologie*. Darmstadt: Wissenschaftliche Buchgesellschaft.

6

Constitutional Issues: 1928–1931

Abstract This chapter continues the focus on 1928 and includes 1929 and concentrates mostly on constitutional issues. This includes Schmitt's essay regarding the guardian of the constitution. But this chapter also addresses the tension between democracy's twin beliefs about freedom and equality. For Schmitt, liberalism's problem is its emphasis on the individual whereas his concern is with the people.

Keywords Constitution • Issues • State • Democracy • Unity

The year 1928 was still a period of relative calm in Germany. Inflation remained mostly under control, street battles tended to be infrequent, and Germany was moving more forcefully to regain its place in world affairs. The year 1929 was totally different; as Carl Schmitt wrote in the "Vorwort" to the 1958 collection of articles on constitutional questions, 1929 saw the beginning of a time of economic and constitutional crises (Schmitt 1958a: 7). In a note written in 1958, Schmitt admitted that that year differed from 1932, just as Bonn was not Weimar. But he maintained that it was worth publishing *Verfassungsrechtliche Aufsätze aus den*

© The Author(s) 2020

C. Adair-Toteff, *Carl Schmitt on Law and Liberalism*, Palgrave Studies in Classical Liberalism, https://doi.org/10.1007/978-3-030-57118-4_6

Jahren 1924–1954 because of their importance and he pointed specifically to the year 1929 as the beginning of a period of great tragedy. To underscore that, he referred to the observation of the state secretary for the ministry of economics—Ernst Trendelenburg who compared the collapse of the New York stock exchange during the last part of October 1929 with the breaking of the windows in Prague in May of 1618. And, that was the beginning of the "Thirty Year War." The constitutional issues appeared to be primarily theoretical and certainly they did not have the impact that the economic crises had. Nonetheless, those were not just damaging, but they were also laying the groundwork for the genuine constitutional crises of 1930–1933. Thus, this chapter and the next share many of the same years, but the focus of each is different. This chapter is centered on constitutional issues and questions; the next one is devoted to the various legal crises which were discussed in German journals and books and were hotly debated in German court rooms.

In terms of Carl Schmitt's personal life, it was somewhat similar to Germany in 1928–1931. The year 1928 was still a rather comfortable time for Schmitt. He was appointed professor of law at the "Handelshochschule" in Berlin in 1928 and his writings were often eagerly awaited. Yet, Schmitt's writings were often criticized by some of the leading scholars. When Schmitt first published "Das Reichsgericht als Hüter der Verfassung," many scholars responded critically, including Hans Kelsen and Joseph Popitz. Kelsen continued to be recognized as one of the leading constitutional theorists and the recent publication of his *Allgemeine Staatslehre* had just helped to substantiate it. Kelsen was and would remain a staunch opponent of Schmitt. Popitz had been the state secretary for finance but had a legal background so his reply to Schmitt was not out of the ordinary. But unlike Kelsen, Popitz became a close friend of Schmitt. In 1958, Schmitt dedicated his *Verfassungsrechtliche Aufsätze* to the memory of Popitz who had died in 1945.

Carl Schmitt's *Verfassungslehre* was not a typical commentary on the Reichsverfassung in comparison to those by Gerhard Anschütz or by Leo Wittmeyer (Anschütz 1933; Wittmeyer 1922). Those two were genuine commentaries: the former was a direct commentary on each of the 181 articles, whereas the latter was organized around the major themes of the constitution's sections. In contrast, Schmitt insisted that his book was neither a commentary nor a series of monographs; instead, he stated that it was a system (Schmitt 2010: XI). As such, it deserves to be treated systematically, but this book is not a commentary on Schmitt's *Verfassungslehre*. It is a work devoted to his ideas about constitutional law and the role it plays in modern liberal democracy. In light of its uniqueness and its significance, the approach taken here will be rather selective.

As is often the case, Schmitt began by emphasizing the many senses of the term "Verfassung" and by noting that people and things have a constitution. Nonetheless, it is used here as a constitution of a state, which he maintains is restricted to the "political unity of a people" ("politische Einheit eines Volkes"). In this, Schmitt has taken issue with three aspects of the traditional approach to the constitution: first, by objecting to the traditional view that a constitution is somehow "fundamental" ("Grund")—whether it is a "fundamental law" ("Grundgesetz") or a "fundamental norm" ("Grundnorm"). And, second, by questioning whether "norm" is even applicable to the concept of a constitution (Schmitt 2010: 3–4). Finally, third is his insistence in differentiating between a constitution and constitutional laws. The latter are laws and are based upon the constitution, but the constitution itself is not a law. Instead, it is a deliberate expression of a political will and it expresses the will of the political unity. His concern is with three notions of constitution: the first concerns the general "political unity and social order" ("politischer Einheit und sozialer Ordnung") which seems to suggest two separate entities, and he insists that the constitution is the "soul" of concrete life. The second is more limited and is restricted to a specific type of "political and social order" ("politischer und sozialer Ordnung") and this is devoted to the domination in each of the traditional forms of state—monarchy, aristocracy, and democracy. The third notion is the "principle of the *dynamic becoming* of the political unity" ("Prinzip des *dynamischen Werdens* der politischen Einheit") in which the notion of the state as static and stationary is replaced by the concept of one with effective power and energy (Schmitt 2010: 5–6. 21). This third sense is linked with Schmitt's notion that the constitution is a type of decision and that the Weimar constitution was the people's decision in favor of democracy and parliament (Schmitt 2010: 23–24). The focus here will be on two major themes: the nature and function of a constitution and the relationship between democratic politics and the modern constitution.

The notion of political unity and social order had pervaded Schmitt's thinking since the end of the First World War, if not before. And, it is a reflection of his great fear of chaos and his deep conviction that the modern liberal order is unsuited to keep it at bay. Regarding the constitution, if it is regarded as a founding document it gains a sense of respect. But this sense of respect is accompanied by a belief in its permanence. It has the sense of being etched in stone; hence, it is resistant to changes. And, any changes made to it must be both minimal and imperative. This sense of reverence and its unchanging form makes it hard for it to adapt to changing circumstances. That is why Schmitt likes the idea of a dynamic becoming. This is linked to his insistence that a constitution is not a legal document but a political one. It is a decision made by the people under extreme circumstances. It is a political decision because it is a rejection of the old legal order and a replacement by a new one (Schmitt 2010: 58). And, this decision was made by the "political unity" ("politische Einheit") of the German "Volk." Furthermore, Schmitt was convinced that this political decision placed all political power in the hands of one person—the leader. In effect, this decision ratified the power of the sovereign dictator. He points to Article 1 in which the Weimar constitution notes that "the state's force is granted by the people" ("Die Staatsgewalt geht vom Volke aus") (Schmitt 2010: 59–60). The fact that this force is derived from the people undercuts the liberal belief that the constitution is a contract. This is partly because a contract is a legal document, and as Schmitt had consistently argued, a constitution is a not a legal document but a political decision. It is also in part because a contract is between two individuals or two groups, whereas the constitution is a decision offered by a single group—the "political unity" (Schmitt 2010: 61–65). Schmitt does admit that there can be legal contracts that are based upon people's agreement but he insists that these are not the same as a constitution. That is because those contracts are founded upon norms and rules, but a constitution is not founded on those (Schmitt 2010: 68–73). Schmitt again maintains that a constitution revolves around the notion of force and that it goes to the issue of political existence. A legal contract is based upon norms but a constitution is predicated upon a single will. In addition, a contract will divide up rights and responsibilities, but the power granted by a constitution is "unified and indivisible" ("einheitlich und unteilbar") (Schmitt 2010: 77, 84).

Schmitt turns his attention to an idea that will become more important in the early 1930s and that is the opposition between legality and legitimacy. Norms are legal and legality can be used to justify norms; however, a constitution is not a norm and it is contradictory to try to use legal means to justify a constitution. That is because a constitution is a rejection of the previous legal order. Hence, the only justification for a constitution is a type of legitimacy and Schmitt argued that there are only two forms of legitimacy—dynastic and democratic. The former rests upon the authority of the monarch but the latter is founded upon the "political unity of a Volk" ("politische Einheit eines Volkes") (Schmitt 2010: 90).

In the third major section Schmitt addresses the relationship between the political standing and the modern constitution and he begins by setting out the fundamentals of modern democracy. Much of this section is of interest to constitutional scholars and much of it is of interest to political theorists. However, there is much to be learned about Schmitt's thinking about modern democracy with respect to law and even liberalism.

Schmitt repeats his notion that the people ("Volk") in a democracy exhibit a principle of identity, that is, "one people" (Schmitt 2010: 223). But he differentiates between a democracy and a republic by noting that the first one is considered positively whereas the second one has had negative connotations since Machiavelli's writings. Once again, democracy is Schmitt's focus and he offers the typical definition of it as the "majority rule" ("Herrschaft der Mehrheit") but it is not always clear what constitutes the majority. Is it represented by public opinion and how does the notion of the majority fit with the notion of freedom? That is because, freedom is a liberal term used to reflect the freedom of the individual. Thus, there is a collision of sorts between the domination by the collective and the freedom of the individual. Plus, there is an additional issue with democracy because it is an "ideal concept" ("Idealbegriff") which is used by the socialists as well as the liberals, thus underscoring the term's variety of senses (Schmitt 2010: 224–225).

And, once more Schmitt highlights the discrepancy between the two cardinal virtues of democracy: "equality" ("Gleichheit") and "freedom" ("Freiheit"). "Freedom" is a political concept but it also has various meanings. It belongs to the essence of democracy but it also has a number of other applications. These include "equality of laws" ("Gleichheit des Gesetzes"), "equality of voting right" ("Gleiches Wahlrecht"), the "general military obligation" ("allgemeine Wehrpflicht"), and the equal access to offices ("gleicher Zugang zu den Ämtern") (Schmitt 2010: 226–227). However, he noted that throughout history, political thinkers have emphasized the concept of equality but have typically restricted its application. Thus, Aristotle believed in equality but only for the Greeks and not for the "barbarians." This notion underwent transformations by the Stoa and then by Thomas and then by Montesquieu and it achieves a prominent role in Rousseau. Yet, "equality" is expressed the strongest by the Jacobin dictatorship (Schmitt 2010: 228–230). And, the Jacobin dictatorship insisted on equality as an expression of the homogeneous state, that is, one "Volk." This is achieved by different methods: by limiting immigration, like what the United States and English countries did. Or it was by the domination of other peoples, like what the colonial powers did. Or it was by the protection of the state and industry by prohibiting foreign influence, as is often accomplished by many nations at war (Schmitt 2010: 231–232). But all of these methods presuppose the unity of the people and that is why Schmitt insists that the central concept of democracy is "Volk" and "*not humanity*" ("*nicht Menschheit*").

Schmitt repeats the assertion in the Weimar constitution that the power of the state is derived from the "Volk" and he insists that that means that the "Volk" is both prior to and above the constitution. Furthermore, he repeats his claim that the founding of the constitution is not a legal move but is a political decision (Schmitt 2010: 238). He clarifies this by stating that a "Volk" exists only in the public sphere and that they are dependent on one another: "no Volk without the public and no public without the Volk" ("Volk und Öffentlichkeit bestehen zusammen; kein Volk ohne Öffentlichkeit und keine Öffentlichkeit ohne Volk") (Schmitt 2010: 243). And, that is because the "Volk" must be present and that it cannot be represented. In this sense, Rousseau was undoubtedly correct. But Schmitt differed from Rousseau and one of the best examples of this was his repeated emphasis on public acclamation. Schmitt argued against the liberalism of Jeremy Bentham because the Englishman insisted on individual secret ballots. However, the individual ballot goes against the fundamental democratic principle of the rule by the "Volk." If each isolated person turns in a secret ballot, then there is no sense of the people voting as a people. In effect, the individual secret ballot eliminates the possibility of the acclamation by the "Volk." It also eliminates the possibility of a "public opinion"—even if a million private individuals shared the same opinion, it would not be a "public opinion." Instead of being a "common will" ("Gemeinwille"), it would only be a sum of private opinions (Schmitt 2010: 245–246). And, Schmitt insisted that modern democracy is the "rule of public opinion" ("Herrschaft der öffentlichen Meinung") and that public opinion is the modern expression of acclamation. He insisted that public opinion is essential and that there can be no democracy or a state without public opinion. Schmitt granted that there have always been those who have sought to direct public opinion, from the ancient Athenian demagogues to the modern American "bosses," but he insisted that as long as there is a "Volk" that can distinguish between "friend" and "fiend" that the concern that the "Volk" can be manipulated is minimized (Schmitt 2010: 247).

It is not that Schmitt was objecting to the notion of a party; he was objecting to the power of the party "boss." In fact, he insisted that democracy cannot exist without political parties and he suggested that the Weimar constitution was not democratic because it did not mention political parties. Furthermore, the party is at least representative of some part of public opinion. This, Schmitt insisted, has been part of public opinion since the eighteenth century. The members of the Enlightenment tended to support an enlightened despot but they recognized that public opinion was a secure guarantee against the misuse of state power. Freedom of the press was necessary, not as an individual legal right, but as a general public political right (Schmitt 2010: 248–249). And, again, Schmitt emphasized that the political principle of democracy was not founded on the individual but on democratic identity; rather than liberalism's inequality, democracy demanded equality. This is indicated by the concept of the "citizen of the state" ("Staatsbürger") which Schmitt insists is a political concept. In a democracy, the person is not a private individual but a citizen ("*citoyen*") (Schmitt 2010: 253). And, all citizens are equal—in terms of appearing before the law, in terms of military duty, in terms of voting, and in terms of appearing before an official (Schmitt 2010: 254–256).

Schmitt turned his attention to democracy and legislating and again maintained that a "democratic legal concept" ("*demokratischer Gesetzesbegriff*") is not a "legal state" concept but is a political concept—one that comes from the power of the people. It is an expression of the will of the "Volk." As he had in *Volksentscheid und Volksbegehren*, Schmitt places an inordinate amount of emphasis on the people's capacity to force political issues through referendums and similar political instruments (Schmitt 2010: 258–259, 262–264).

When Schmitt turned his attention to the relationship between democracy and the government, he again stressed the importance of the immediacy of the "Volk." That is why he minimizes the need for representation because the "Volk" is a "political unity" ("politische Einheit") and it represents the application of the democratic principle of identity (Schmitt 2010: 269). The notion of identity plays a role in the administration and in law; in the first case, there is a tension between the people and the administrators but this can be relieved if the administrators remember that they are also members of the "Volk." Schmitt reemphasizes that in a democracy the "Volk" is a political unity and is not composed of a group of voters. The situation is more problematic with respect to a judge because there is a real tension between the judge as an independent arbiter of the law and as a member of the political class. Although it is unclear, it seems that Schmitt's suggestion for alleviating this tension is to talk about "Volks-Justiz" and what he appears to have in mind is the overlapping of the judge's decision with the legal sense of the "Volk" (Schmitt 2010: 274–276).

Schmitt spent a fair amount of effort in discussing two types of government—the monarchy or the rule by the one and the aristocracy or the rule by the few. This discussion would be of interest to the political philosopher but is irrelevant here. But what is clearly relevant is his examination of the third traditional type of government or the rule by the many. And, for Schmitt, this meant the parliamentarian system of government. This again prompts him to take up the opposition between liberalism and democracy. The former believes in the doctrine of private property and the state's legal doctrine whereas the latter holds to the two principles of freedom and equality. Schmitt further distinguishes between the two by pointing out that liberalism presupposes "ownership" ("Besitz") whereas democracy presupposes "education" ("Bildung"). The former is an individual matter and as it is a matter of the interest of the owner, it cannot be represented; in contrast, the latter is a general quality and as such is a national issue. That is why Schmitt insisted that education and reason belong to the entire nation and why he claimed that "the concept of nation is an educational concept" ("der Begriff der Nation ist ein Bildungsbegriff") (Schmitt 2010: 307–311).

The parliament is the place where public discussion regarding political opinions can occur, at least ideally. Ideally, parliament represents the entire nation and ideally all of its proceedings are visible to the public. However, Schmitt maintains that modern parliament has lost that manner of representation and has chosen to avoid public scrutiny. Parliament is no longer the place where rational arguments prevail and is now the place where individual interests dominate. Furthermore, parliament is no longer the venue where open discussions lead to open decisions but is the place where committees decide and then announce their decisions, which tend to be driven by the hidden party influence (Schmitt 2010: 317–319).

The remainder of this section is devoted to the historical development of the parliamentarian system in Europe and culminates in Schmitt's critique of the parliamentary system of the Weimar constitution. The constitution is ostensibly a balanced one with the executive and the legislative branches having equal weight. In addition, the "Reichspräsident" is supposed to be an impartial and neutral power—an "objective" man and not a "Führer" (Schmitt 2010: 350–351). But in reality this is mostly for show and Schmitt documents this by pointing out that during the 1922 conflict between Bavaria and the Reich, "Reichspräsident" Ebert sided with the Reich, thereby undermining the claim of the Weimar constitution that the "Reichspräsident" is chosen by the entire "Volk" and is mandated to represent all of it (Schmitt 2010: 350–351). It is fitting that Schmitt chose to end the section on the politic part in the modern constitution by criticizing the Weimar constitution; thus, showing that his *Verfassungslehre* was never intended to be a doctrine of constitution but was a political treatise. That is because for Schmitt, almost everything was political.

In honor of the tenth anniversary of the Weimar constitution a number of constitutional scholars wrote articles for the occasion. One of the scholars was Carl Schmitt, but if he had intended his article "Zehn Jahre Reichsverfassung" to honor the Weimar constitution, it was a very strange way to do so. Instead of praising the constitution, he criticized numerous aspects of it. These ranged from the critical remarks about Hugo Preuss' original intentions to the multiple changes during those ten years to the difficulties that Germany encountered in 1929. He noted that it is hard to consider the situation in 1929 compared to the summer a decade earlier. There had been so many political and economic changes that had altered the meaning and significance of the Weimar constitution. Many, if not most, of the changes affected the second half of the constitution—the part devoted to the fundamental rights and duties of the German citizens ("Grundrechte und Grundpflichten der Deutschen"). Hugo Preuss had originally discounted the need for such a section but when it was included it was quite extensive—containing almost 70 articles. What was more interesting were the changes in the interpretations of these articles and how they became more crucial. Rather than being interpreted as "mere programs" or "simple proclamations" these were quickly and significantly altered. Schmitt pointed to the time during which inflation subsided and a period of stabilization began that many of these changes occurred. One of the most crucial occurred in 1925 when the rights of the German citizens were further cemented by a particular judicial decision (Schmitt 1958b: 34–35). However, these changes did not solidify the unity of the Weimar constitution. Instead, the attempts at reaching a compromise with the liberal-individualistic people and the Catholic-natural law adherents failed. And, the socialistic inclined groups meant that the changes in constitutional interpretation became even more fragmented and at odds with one another. They led to interpretations of a "grotesque manner" ("groteske Weise") and to all kinds of differences of opinion (Schmitt 1958b: 96–87). Schmitt singled out Article 76 which was devoted to referendums and changes to the constitution. If it was regarded as a minor revision it was one thing. But if it was considered as a significant alteration then that was another thing. Because then it would be undermining the foundation of the entire constitution. In essence, the second half of the constitution was now in the hands of the German courts and its future depended upon the German "science of law" ("Rechtswissenschaft"). And, Schmitt concluded that in the hands of the bureaucrats and lawyers that the second half of the Weimar constitution may very well be the means for the private egoists to misuse and abuse. Thus, the very part that was supposed to guarantee the fundamental rights of the German citizens might be used to oppress the German "Volk" (Schmitt 1958b: 39–40).

Hugo Preuss was the author of the Weimarer Reichsverfassung but he was neither well-liked nor very respected by every German. Some accused him of diminishing Germany's place in the world while others suspected his Jewishness was harming Germany itself. But when he died unexpectedly in 1925 most Germans mourned his passing and a number of scholars wrote tributes. Whether one regards Schmitt's "Hugo Preuß. Sein Staatsbegriff und seine Stellung in der Deutschen Staatslehre" as a tribute may be a simple matter of opinion. It began as a lecture in 1930 which was almost five years after Preuss' death. And, the portrait that Schmitt paints of him is not of a revered statesman but as a political outsider. One may be inclined to wonder how much of this portrait is a projection of Schmitt's own positions. This is immediately indicated by Schmitt's claim that all political concepts stem from concrete oppositions, because without an opposite, these concepts would be senseless abstractions. In addition, these political concepts gain power from the more definite contrasts, and one of these is the contrast between "Freunde" and "Feind." By having a concrete antithesis, the concept is rescued from the daily polemical "word-fog" ("Wortnebel") (Schmitt 2016b: 164). While most commentators would have assumed that Preuss was a member of the government, Schmitt suggested that he was a long-time member of the opposition, one who was a polemical writer. One of Preuss' sleight of hands was to insist that he was a-political, whereas he claimed that his opponent was being extremely political. This was especially true with respect to Preuss' legal writings and that rather than being purely juristic documents they were really political pamphlets. This is also apparent in Preuss' notion of the state as an organic entity, that is, the personification of the state. This is an indication of Preuss' liberalism and adherence to democracy, but it is also a hint of the multiple meanings and evasions that come with the word "organic" (Schmitt 2016b: 167–169).

Schmitt listed seven traits that accompanied Germany's nineteenth-century doctrine of the "organic" state. These are: (1) it is not mechanical, (2) it does not come from outside, (3) it does not come from above, (4) it is not forceful, (5) it is not atomistic, (6) it is not particular, and (7) it is not passive and inactive. But these are all negative traits; instead, "organic" can mean almost anything and that is why German political thinkers from conservative to liberal all claimed that their theories of state were "organic" throughout the nineteenth century and into the twentieth century (Schmitt 2016b: 169–175).

The "critical" moment comes in the history of a word when it has a new opponent, and for "organic" it came for Preuss during November of 1918. That is when he moved from being between Left and Right and began to think about a new constitution. It also gave him the opportunity to address the notion of equality. The liberal state likes to think of itself as neutral but then it is confronted with the issue of inequality. These are two points which Schmitt had made in the past—that liberalism and democracy are not only not the same but that they are not even compatible. That is because the former accepts the notion of inequality whereas the latter rejects it. And, he cites no less an authority than Max Weber for confirmation. Preuss' answer is similar—that the state and the law have different approaches to equality: that all must be regarded as being equal under the law but must be treated as individuals by the state. But Schmitt traces this difference back to the French Revolution and the demand for equality and then notes the Hegelian origins of the organic conception of the state as well as the concept of "Geist" ("spirit") in history (Schmitt 2016b: 171–174, 178–180, 182). However, Schmitt saw in Preuss a different type of spirit—one that also recognized that political concepts are polemical concepts. And, he praised him for having the right spirit of independence that was required to write the Weimar constitution (Schmitt 2016b: 184). How much this picture corresponds to the actual Hugo Preuss is best left to the Preuss scholar. But it seems rather clear that much of what Schmitt wrote about Preuss is an accurate reflection of Schmitt's own convictions.

Carl Schmitt published the original version of his "guardian of the constitution" as an article in 1929. It carried the title "Das Reichsgericht als Hüter der Verfassung," and while it appears as if this article would be a treatise on the issue of protecting the constitution, an examination of it proves that it is more of a political pamphlet. Schmitt noted that while most constitutions have had some provision discussing protection, the Weimar constitution does not. He noted that historically different courts were regarded as the proper guardian of the constitution and he mentioned the "state court" ("Staatsgerichtshof") and the "constitutional court" ("Verfassungsgerichtshof") as two of them, but he argued that much of their duty was to determine whether the laws were constitutional and that they were not acting as the protectors of the constitution. In other words, these courts were resolving legal conflicts and they did so by the means of clarification (Schmitt 1958c: 63–65). In contrast, the issue of who should be the custodian of the constitution is not a simple matter of clarification but is far more complex. He adds that it is impossible to provide a full answer in a brief article but he believes that he can point in the right direction for an answer. Part of the complexity of the matter is that one needs to determine from which side the danger to the constitution comes—the executive or the legislative branches. And, part of the problem is that scholars tend to regard the constitution as another law and that it is a norm. But Schmitt insists again that the constitution is neither a law nor a norm, but is a political decision concerning the manner and form of political existence; hence, the decision regarding who is the guardian of the constitution is a fundamentally political decision and not an ordinary legal one. Hence, it is wrong to speak about "constitutional justice" ("Verfassungsjustiz"). He explained that the constitution does not fall in the area of state activity, by which he meant decisions regarding legal conflicts and the possibility of penalties (Schmitt 1958c: 69–73). Schmitt argued that it is incorrect to think of the constitution as a law because it is not the object of a court process. Nor is it correct to regard the constitution as a type of contract. Both instances require an independent judge to hear both sides and then make an impartial judicial pronouncement. But the case of a constitutional issue is not a legal one, but a political one. Thus, to place a constitutional question, which is a political one, at the bench of a non-political judge would lead to "absurd results" (Schmitt 1958c: 74). He complained in a footnote that Kelsen thought of the constitution as a contract because he believed that it was a type of compromise. And, Kelsen thought of the state as an ongoing compromise. He blames Kelsen's formalistic and normative thinking for leading him to ignore the fact that the constitution is a political document (Schmitt 1958c: 76, note 31). Thus, the judge who decides the law must be independent of all political decisions, but it is the legislator who makes the law which is based primarily upon political decisions. The judge makes legal determinations but the legislator makes political decisions. And, Schmitt clarifies this by noting that the judge is not an "expert witness" ("Gutachter") and he warns that the combination of witnessing and judicial activity would lead to an unclear mixture when they need to be kept separate (Schmitt 1958c: 77–79, 81).

Schmitt insisted that the Weimar constitution was a constitution like those that separate the power of force from the power of decision and that the Weimar constitution was a fundamental, political decision. However, a court does not determine political decisions but deals with legal decisions (Schmitt 1958c: 88–89). And, he concludes with some observations regarding the proper guardian of the constitution. He suggested that the question about the possibility of a judicial constitutional protector cannot be determined solely in conjunction with "constitutional doctrine" ("Verfassunslehre"), but must also be addressed by the "general doctrine of the state" ("allgemeine Staatslehre"). That is because of the possibility of using force against the state and its constitution. However, Schmitt is convinced that if the state maintains its "political unity," then that it is not a legal question but is a political one. In Schmitt's opinion, it is a problem that many legal scholars are too convinced that these are legal questions and issues of norms; thus, they are either unable or too willful to recognize these issues as political issues. Thus, the question about protecting the constitution cannot be solved by judges and legal rulings; rather, it can be only resolved by people making political decisions. After all, the constitution was never a legal document but a founding political declaration (Schmitt 1958c: 98–100).

Johannes Popitz replied with "Wer ist Hüter der Verfassung" and it is to Schmitt's credit that he included it in *Verfassungsrechtliche Aufsätze*. Popitz suggested that the words "Der Hüter der Verfassung" sounded earnest and weighty and he noted that they raise the issue of the duties of the citizens toward their constitution. But he wondered whether the "right believers" are the proper guardians of the constitution and he questioned whether the idea of the enemy and the conviction that the state must be a unity are the correct ways to approach this matter. Is it not an issue for the people themselves? Is it not their duty to be the guardians of the constitution by obeying and protecting it? And, Popitz observed that maybe the danger to the constitution does not come from the citizens but from the officials who are entrusted with carrying out the constitutional orders. It is not the populace which has access to the constitutional instruments to alter and abolish the constitution but the officers of the constitutionally recognized government. For it is not the citizens who can invoke Article 49 but the legally elected officials (Popitz 1958: 101–102).

Popitz delineated how Schmitt believed that the state fundamentally changed when it converted from an administrative state ("Verwaltungsstaat") to a welfare state ("Wohlfahrtsstaat") and even more so when it turned into a party-based state ("Partiestaat") and an economic state ("Wirtschaftsstaat") (Popitz 1958: 102–103). He pointed to Schmitt's complaint about the number of voices in the competing parties and the liberal emphasis on the individual in economics. And, he noted that Schmitt's dark picture raised the question whether there even could be a legal protector of the constitution because of the collision between what the constitution demanded and what the government wanted (Popitz 1958: 103–104). This is apparent during normal years, but Schmitt was discussing what would happen during abnormal times: "But who is the guardian of the constitution in this danger-threatening condition?" ("Wer aber ist Hüter der Verfassung in diesem gefahrdrohenden Zustand?") (Popitz 1958: 104). In Popitz' mind, there is no question that the Reichspräsident is the guardian of the constitution because this result accords with the democratic principles upon which the Weimar constitution is founded. And, it is the Reichspräsident who has been chosen by the people and who represents the "non-party objectivity and neutrality" ("unparteiliche Objektivität und Neutralität"). This had been amply demonstrated by the first two presidents, but Schmitt wonders about the third. Popitz concludes with the comment that this is not the place to discuss the doubts that Schmitt's writing raises and the expansions that it demands, but it does call attention to the important question of what is a state and who should lead it (Popitz 1958: 105).

Most of this chapter dealt with scholarly questions and it remains mostly abstract and theoretical: what is the nature and function of a constitution and what can be learned from the ten-year history of the Weimar constitution? What is the function of the Reichspräsident and who should be considered as the guardian of the constitution? Scholars debated these and other constitutional issues with little or no practical effects. This would not be the case with the constitutional crises which developed in the years 1930, 1931, and 1932.

References

Anschütz, Gerhard (1933)[1921] *Die Verfassung des Deutschen Reichs. vom 11. August 1919*. Berlin: Verlag von Georg Stilke. 14. Auflage.

Popitz, Johannes (1958)[ ] "Wer ist Hüter der Verfassung?" In Schmitt 1958a. 101–105.

Schmitt, Carl (1958a) *Verfassungsrechtliche Aufsätze aus den Jahren 1924–1954. Materialien zu einer Verfassungslehre*. Berlin: Duncker & Humblot

Schmitt, Carl (1958b)[1929] "Zehn Jahre Reichsverfassung." In Schmitt 1958a. 34–40.

Schmitt, Carl (1958c)[1929] "Das Reichsgericht als Hüter der Verfassung." In Schmitt 1958a. 63–101.

Schmitt, Carl (2010)[1928] *Verfassungslehre*. Berlin: Duncker & Humblot. Zehnte Auflage.

Schmitt, Carl (2016a)[1931] *Der Hüter der Verfassung*. Berlin: Duncker & Humblot. Fünfte Auflage.

Schmitt, Carl (2016b)[1930] "Hugo Preuß. Sein Staatsbegriff und seine Stellung in der deutschen Staatslehre." In Schmitt 2016a. 164–184.

Wittmeyer, Leo (1922) *Die Weimarer Reichsverfassung*. Tübingen: Verlag von J.C.B. Mohr (Paul Siebeck).

7

Constitutional Chaos and Political Turmoil: 1930–1932

Abstract This chapter covers the years 1930–1932 and that means examining a range of Schmitt's writings. These include some rather bland legal works like *Legalität und Legitimität*, but it also includes his polemical tracts, such as *Der Begriff des Politischen*. Thus, it covers the issues of legality as well as legitimacy, and it also includes his continuing assaults on the deficiencies of liberal democracy in general and of the Weimar constitution in particular. Finally, this period seems to mark Schmitt's transition from legal scholar to party partisan and it culminates in his attacks on law and liberalism.

Keywords Constitution • Chaos • Turmoil • Order • Legality

The years 1930, 1931, and 1932 were turbulent years throughout much of the world and even more so in Germany. The political crises in Germany not only grew in number but also in intensity, culminating in the political collapse of the Weimar government. Throughout this time Carl Schmitt led almost a dual life—outwardly politically involved in writing and tracing, inwardly uneasy and not always self-assured. During

© The Author(s) 2020

C. Adair-Toteff, *Carl Schmitt on Law and Liberalism*, Palgrave Studies in Classical Liberalism, https://doi.org/10.1007/978-3-030-57118-4_7

this time, he continued to be an "outsider," but after January 30, 1933 he would be an "insider"—not just as the "crown jurist" but in Reinhard Mehring's phrase "in the stomach of Leviathan" ("im Bauch des Leviathan") (Mehring 2009: 303). This invocation of Hobbes is an indication of Schmitt's later investigation into what he perceived as Hobbes' failure to understand the nature of the state in his 1937 book on Hobbes. Mehring devotes almost ten pages to this portion of Schmitt's life and it is certainly worth reading (Mehring 2009: 380–389). But given that that episode occurred later, it will not be addressed here.

In 1930, Carl Schmitt published a brief essay in the journal *Kant-Studien*. Its appearance in that journal is noteworthy for a number of reasons. First, *Kant-Studien* was the official journal of the *Kant Gesellschaft* and was founded in 1897 by the noted Kant scholar Hans Vaihinger. Vaihinger had first made his name as the author of a massive two-volume commentary devoted to the first fifty pages of Kant's *Critique of Pure Reason*, but he never finished it because of failing eyesight. Nonetheless, he was one of the first philosophers to take Friedrich Nietzsche seriously and he worked to develop his own philosophy of "as if" ("als-ob"). By 1930 he was associated with Nietzsche's sister and was encouraging people to read both his own philosophy as well as that of Nietzsche. Second, *Kant-Studien* had been intended to be a journal focusing on Kant's transcendental philosophy and had for the most part refrained from publishing political essays. Third, Schmitt's article "Staatsethik und pluralistischer Staat" was a polemic against almost everything Kant had believed in. As a major contributor to the German Enlightenment ("Aufklärung"), Kant believed in reason, tolerance, and moderation. His ethics were formalistic and his view of the state was rather liberal. These were all positions that Schmitt decried and he criticized many of them in this essay.

Schmitt intended not only to defend the notion of the state; he wanted to glorify it. That is why he began by objecting to those scholars like Ernest Barker who wrote about "the discredited state" and those like some French thinkers who declared that "[t]he state is dead" ("Der Staat ist tot") (Schmitt 1988: 133). The state, according to Schmitt, is alive, but is misinterpreted and he lays much of the blame for this on Kant and his "liberal individualism" as well as his formalistic ethics of the state. He counters that Hegel's conception of the state was a vast improvement over that of Kant, and that is because Hegel conceived of the state as a unity and that it encompassed the ethics of the state as a whole. Kant's intellectual heirs include not just Hegel, who moved away from him, but the modern political thinkers who believe in pluralism. Again, Schmitt has Harold Laski in mind and he objects to Laski's conception of the state as something similar to a type of association. This conception leads to a "plurality of loyalty" because one owes allegiance to many different groups—the social club, the worker's union, the religious group, as well as the state. And, Schmitt attacks the philosophical foundations of Laski's pluralism which he believes to be William James' Pragmatism. In his conception of James' philosophy, Schmitt believes that James has countered the unity of the state and that the state is not an ideal but a compilation of differing values. This is why the state appears in different guises—as a mere social group, as an agglomerate of different people, as something similar to a union, as something like a church, or as simply a group which shares many of the same interests. But regardless of the variation, this is a compromise and is not a unity (Schmitt 1988: 136–137, 142). Yet, historically, the unity of the state was the highest value, from Plato to Hegel. And, like the Roman Catholic Church it was monistic and universalistic. In contrast, pluralism devalues the unity and commends the single individual. Yet, it also speaks in terms of humanity—but Schmitt reminds us of Proudhon's observation "Who says humanity, wants to deceive" ("Wer Menscheit sagt, will betrügen") (Schmitt 1988: 138, 143). Laski and others who promote pluralism are not talking about the state, but about society. But society is made up of various and competing groups as well as being composed of individuals who have their own interests. In conclusion, Schmitt turns to Kant and his formalistic ethics. Schmitt objects to Kant's notion of the state as an individual law giver and the idea that a constitution is a kind of agreement. But he really objects to the conception of the state as a pluralistic society and the belief in norms. In its place, Schmitt insists that the state is an ethical unity and that its citizens have a "state-ethical duty" ("staatsethiche Pflicht")—"namely, the duty to the state" ("nämlich, die Pflicht zum Staat") (Schmitt 1988: 144–145). Whereas most of Schmitt's fellow constitutional scholars believed in a liberal and protective government, Schmitt was increasingly committed to a central and strong state. In his version of the state, the constitution was not as important as who governed over it. Hence, Schmitt returned to the question regarding who should be the guardian of the constitution.

The book *Der Hüter der Verfassung* has little resemblance either to the "Staatsethik und pluralistischer Staat" or to the essay version "Das Reichsgericht als Hüter der Verfassung." The differences are not just in length but also in tone. The book leaves aside most of the polemical tone of the essays and is far more of a scholarly treatise; thus, it is similar to the *Verfassungslehre*. As such, it does not warrant much discussion here. But Schmitt repeats and modifies some of the charges that he had previously made. These include his assertion that the history of German law had given rise to a misguided notion of law. This was the idea that law was neutral and that judges were impartial decision makers. In this, German law was attempting to duplicate the Anglo-American conception of the "due process of the law" (Schmitt 2016: 35–38). He also repeats the claim that laws and norms apply only in normal times. And, while the situation in 1930 seemed less critical than in the early 1920s, it was by no means a stable one (Schmitt 2016: 45). He also repeats his criticism regarding the constitution as a legal contract. First, it is not a contract between two entities but is a foundational political document. Second, the issue is irrelevant with regard to the specific issue of the guardian of the constitution because a norm cannot safeguard another norm, nor can one law be the protector of another law (Schmitt 2016: 53, 60–63; 40–43). If there is to be an answer to the question of the proper guardian of the constitution, Schmitt insisted that the question had to be removed from a discussion about laws and norms and had to be addressed in its proper forum—that is, the realm of politics (Schmitt 2016: 48–49). And, that means addressing three political concepts.

Of Schmitt's three political concepts, one is familiar—pluralism—but the other two are new—polycraty and federalism. However, he maintains that they are related in the sense that all three are in opposition to a unified and single state (Schmitt 2016: 71). Schmitt addressed the three in order. Previously, German constitutional law distinguished between state and society: the state was the political power and society was composed of economic, religious, and social powers. Whereas there was plurality in society, there was unity in the state (Schmitt 2016: 73). The problem arose when the monarchy was overthrown and the parliamentarian system introduced because then the government was assumed to resemble society. In other words, what had been a single state was transformed into a plurality of voices. Furthermore, this parliament was liberal, which meant that it was founded on the liberal notions that law was contractual, that the free market dominated, and that citizens were entitled to the whole group of individual freedoms, including freedom of opinion, freedom of competition, and freedom of ownership. In essences, this was the liberal, non-interventionist state—which was not really even a state. This was parliamentarian pluralism (Schmitt 2016: 78–81, 87, 90).

Polycraty is the economic form of pluralism and Schmitt regarded Popitz as the scholar who discussed it the most. This is the notion that there is an abundance of individual groups and Popitz noted that Germany had 17 states, 65,000 communities, 7427 health insurers, 106 vocational unions, and 35 invalid insurance institutions. Each of these represented a wide variety of voices, and just as parliamentarianism lead to pluralism, it also led to the intensive development of the state as an "economic state" ("Wirtschaftsstaat") (Schmitt 2016: 92–94).

Federalism was the parliamentarian development of different territorial voices. It is a form of decentralization and it is intended to further the economic development of the individual territories and to ensure its political plurality (Schmitt 2016: 95–96). Thus, pluralism is found in the type of politics, the type of economics, and the type of government. Having set out the forms of plurality, Schmitt attempted to address them and to point to a solution to the question regarding the true guardianship of the constitution. He commented that the German constitution was not an "economic constitution" ("Wirtschaftsverfassung") but that the economic powers tended to ignore the actual German constitution and that is because they put a premium on neutrality (Schmitt 2016: 96, 100–103). However, Schmitt objected to all of the words which indicated impartiality—"neutrality, de-politicalizing, and objectivity" ("Neutralität, Entpolitisierung, und Sachlichkeit") (Schmitt 2016: 108). And, he objected to the reliance on "impartiality" to foster the reluctance to make political decisions. This impartiality has serious repercussions; Schmitt maintained that "[t]he flight out of politics is the flight out of the state" ("Die Flucht aus der Politik ist die Flucht aus dem Staat"

(Schmitt 2016: 111). For Schmitt politics is not neutral so he lays out eight senses of neutrality—four negative: (1) it is non-interventionist, (2) it is a technical means for planning, (3) it offers the same chance, and (4) it provides parity. In each of these cases, it does not really do anything. In contrast, the positive four appear to do something: (1) it provides the basis for norms, (2) it ensures that the basis is not egotistical but is factual, (3) it offers an opposition to anything that relativizes, and (4) it seems to provide a security from outside dangers (Schmitt 2016: 111–115).

Having enumerated the eight different types of neutrality, Schmitt returned to his theme of politics. He insisted that impartiality hurts the political state, so it makes no sense to weaken the state more in the hopes that those measures would strengthen it. He again emphasizes that to think of the state as some neutral legal organization is to make a mistake—and one with negative consequences for it. Instead, Schmitt insists that the state is an expression of the will of the "Volk" and that is what underscores the validity of the state. As he had done in the past, he again insists that the democratic expression of this will is through "agreement and acclamation" ("Zustimmung und Akklamation"). And, the most visible example of these measures is the Reichspräsident (Schmitt 2016: 115–116). Schmitt returned to one of his favorite themes, and that is Paragraph 2 of Article 48 of the Weimar Reichsverfassung. It was a favorite then because it focused on the state of emergency; later it was a favorite because of the extraordinary powers it grants the Reichspräsident (Schmitt 2016: 119–121, 130–131).

In the third and final part of the *Hüter der Verfassung* Schmitt returned to the issue of neutrality and how it connected to his claim that the Reichspräsident is the true guardian of the constitution. He repeats his observation that the notion of neutrality is based upon the French Revolution and its subsequent adoption by the liberal groups in their struggle against the restoration. It was an attempt to be a "neutral third" which was intended to be situated between the forces on the Right and those on the Left (Schmitt 2016: 133–137). However, the Weimar Reichsverfassung has provided the Reichspräsident with a different position—he is chosen by the people to represent the people. In this sense, his election transcends party politics and he is neutral. But Schmitt insisted that the Reichspräsident's neutrality is fundamentally different than the liberal belief. Instead, it is a single entity representing the people as a political unity. This was the case with Ebert and it is the case with Hindenburg. (Schmitt 2016: 139–142). It is the mistake of liberal thinkers like John Stuart Mill to believe that the government should be "balanced" and is intended to mediate (Schmitt 2016: 143–144). In Germany, the government does not need to either be balanced or to mediate because the head of it is the Reichspräsident who has been chosen by the "Volk" and is the head of the "political unity." Because he has been elected by the "Volk" and is charged with securing its interest, the Reichspräsident is the democratically chosen "guardian of the constitution" ("Hüter der Verfassung") (Schmitt 2016: 149, 158–159).

The circumstances which led to the implementation of Article 48 Paragraph 2 of the Weimar constitution are lengthy and disputed. So is the conduct of the Reich as well as the court which provided the decision which justified the Reich's actions. To give an account of all of this is both beyond my capabilities and beyond the scope of this book. Accordingly, the focus will be directed to Carl Schmitt's participation in so far as it has a connection to his criticisms regarding law and liberalism. As much as he was a key player in the legal proceedings, his role is often magnified. In reality, he was one of a number of legal professors who gave testimony and he spoke five times.[1] Before addressing his comments, there needs to be some context provided.

In 1930, the Reich had a relatively stable parliament largely composed of center and left of center parties. By 1932, the centrist parties had lost their majority and the elected members came from the far left and from the center and from the far right. But in Berlin proper, the Prussian government was inclined toward the left which resulted in tension between the Prussian government and the Reich government. Things reached a boiling point on July 20, 1932, when the Reichspräsident von Hindenburg and the Reichskanzler von Papen declared that the Prussian government needed to be dissolved and that all governmental powers would be taken

[1] Schmitt spoke as a representative of the Reich, and although he only spoke five times, he was occasionally invoked. For example, Professor Peters argued at length that Schmitt's arguments against the Weimar constitution were faulty. However, the presiding judge maintained that Peters' objections and even Schmitt's writings were not germane to the case (Preussen 1976: 56–60).

over by the Reich. The ostensible reason was that the Prussian government was no longer willing or able to control the demonstrators and put a stop to the political chaos. The Reich argued that the Bolsheviks were allowed to riot, but in actuality it was the Nazi party members who were more responsible for the unrest. However, the Reich government believed that it could control the Nazis and it moved against Prussia. This was the "Prussian hit" ("Preussenschlag"). The legal justification for this move was the invocation of Article 48 and the formal documentation was published five days later.

The Prussian government was dissolved, but several of its members filed court papers declaring that the Reich's actions went against the Weimar constitution. The case was conducted during the five days of October from 10th to the 14th and then on Monday the 17th. The decision in favor of the Reich was delivered on October 25th.

Carl Schmitt's focus throughout his writings in the 1920s was almost exclusively about Article 46 Paragraph 2, but as the proceedings demonstrate, the Reich lawyers invoked not just Paragraph 2, but also Paragraph 1 (Preussen 1976: IX, 124–285). Schmitt spoke only one time regarding Paragraph 1 and that was in response to Gerhard Anschütz' comments about that Paragraph. Anschütz spoke often and at length, which was not surprising since he was the author of the commentary on the Weimar constitution that was published in a large number of editions. Schmitt did what he often did, which was to emphasize the politics of the constitution and did so here by pointing out that a "huge amount of political capital" ("ungeheures politisches Kapital") was invested into Article 48. But he also took issue with the legal side and he did so by objecting to Anschütz' claim that the Reich was involved in an execution of an act. In contrast, Schmitt insisted that that implies that the Reich was acting when, in fact, the Reich was simply reacting. And, it was reacting to the need to fulfill the duties that the Prussian government was unwilling or unable to fulfill. Furthermore, the specific duty that the Prussian government was not fulfilling was the protection ("Schutz") of its citizens. Since the safety of citizens is one of the most important duties of any government, then it was necessary for the Reich to take these measures. Schmitt argued that this was true throughout history, and it was true in July of 1932 (Preussen 1976: 130–133).

As Article 48 Paragraph 1 indicates, the Reichspräsident can take any measure, including force, to ensure that a "Land" fulfills its duty. However, Schmitt was not all that concerned with duties; rather, his concern had always been and was then with "public security and order" ("öffentliche Sicherheit und Ordnung") which Schmitt insisted was "the first and most important obligation of a state" ("die erste und wichtigste Verpflichtung des Landes") (Preussen 1976: 133). Schmitt returned to his theme when the discussion moved to Paragraph 2 and he maintained that the decision to intervene was necessitated by both legal and political factors. And, he argued that the factors often rest upon the nature of the problem. He noted that the lack of order would not have been the same problem if it had been occurring in the smaller "Länder," but that it had occurred in Prussia which was the largest. He observed that it is well-known that one does not shoot cannons at sparrows ("Man schießt bekanntlich nicht mit Kanonen nach Spatzen") but that the danger here to "public security and order" ("öffentliche Sicherheit und Ordnung") was great enough to warrant the measures (Preussen 1976: 289–290).

Friday, the 14th of October was the fifth day of the trial and after the "Reich Court President" ("Reichsgerichtspräsident") Dr. Bumke opened the proceedings at 9:30 in the morning; the first person to address the court was Carl Schmitt for the Reich. He promised not to misuse the first hour of that day's proceedings and directed his attention to the concept of limits ("Grenzen"). He acknowledged Anschütz' previous day's defense of limits, but argued that their relevance was diminished in cases where chaos has exploded. In such cases the legal government has the right and the duty to make the decision to suspend those limits. In such cases, the legal authority has the right to dictatorial powers (Preussen 1976: 311–314, 316–317). Schmitt specifically invokes the notion of war and the right to employ all necessary means to counter the enemy—including the use of force. Schmitt concluded by insisting that Article 48 Paragraph 2 authorized the Reich to take those appropriate measures on July 20, 1932 (Preussen 1976: 319–322).

Schmitt spoke later in the day and after clarifying a number of minor legal points, he turned his attention to his main issue. That issue was the relationship between Reich and Land, in this case, Prussia. He reminded the court that the Prussian government could no longer function properly because it was composed of communists and of Nazis. This governmental failure was manifested not only in the Prussian parliament but on Prussian streets. If Prussia's government lacked competency, then it constitutionally fell to the Reich to use its competency for the restoration of "public *security and order*" ("öffentliche *Sicherheit und Ordnung*") (Preussen 1976: 350–353). And, Schmitt again reminded the court that during the war, extraordinary circumstances required extraordinary measures. Schmitt not only invoked Germany's history of dealing with exceptional circumstances. He also illustrated his points by looking to the histories of Switzerland and the United States. Regarding the US, Schmitt reminded his listeners that there was no opposition between the states and the federal government: "state power in Feindshaft zu der federal power" (sic), and that meant "[t]he supremacy of the national power—in this case the power of the federal government" ("Die Supremität der nationalen Macht—in diesem Falle der Bundesmacht"). Finally, he mentioned that one of the previous speakers had mentioned the necessity of the national point of view and he explicitly referred to the great constitutional expert Georg Jellinek. In line with Jellinek's thinking, Schmitt insisted that his interpretation of Article 48 was also grounded upon the "national position" ("nationalen Standpunkt") (Preussen 1976: 355).

On Monday, October 17th, Carl Schmitt spoke again and he once again emphasized that what the Reich did was a political act as well as a legal one. He further noted that there can be only one type of legal trial—either a Land counters the Reich or the Reich counters a Land. In this case, Prussia had claimed that it has been damaged, yet as Schmitt pointed out it, Prussia did not disappear and it has a government (Preussen 1976: 466–467). The problem was of Prussia's own making because it was not fulfilling its highest duty to provide "public security and order" ("öffentliche Sicherheit und Ordnung"). In other words, it showed that it was unable to function as a Land. Thus, the only question is whether the Reich had the power, but that was easily answered under Article 48. There are two words which were often said—the first was the question of who is the guardian of the constitution but here Schmitt insisted that it was obvious that this court ("Reichsgerichtshof") is the true guardian of the constitution. The second word that was often said was concerned with Prussia's "honor" ("Ehre"), but again Schmitt maintained that it was the

Prussian government which contributed to the loss of honor. Instead, it was Reichspräsident von Hindenburg who not only secured Prussia's honor and dignity, but is the true guardian of the honor of the Reich (Preussen 1976: 469).

The decision came on October 25th and it was not much of a surprise. The court noted that the Reich intervened in order to prevent a civil war (Preussen 1976: 500). The court justified the legal intervention by appealing to Article 48 Paragraph 2 about the need for "public security and order" ("öffentliche Sicherheit und Ordnung") (Preussen 1976: 513, 515, 517). Prussia had failed, and the Reich was forced to act; thus, it had constitutional justification in so doing.

During 1932, Carl Schmitt published two books, both of which created controversy. Outwardly, they appeared to be fundamentally different—*Legalität und Legitimität* was a legal treatise whereas *Der Begriff des Politischen* was a political pamphlet. But both were controversial: the first one because of Schmitt's devaluation of law and the second one because of his "*Freund-Feind*" ("friend-foe") distinction. But both cemented his reputation as a uniquely political legal scholar.

Legalität und Legitimität is composed of a brief introduction, a large first part, an even larger second part, and a conclusion. The differences in lengths seem to reflect Schmitt's varying degrees of interest. In the introduction, he distinguishes between the legal system of a legislating state and various other types. He contended that such a distinction was warranted by the current crises, just as the distinction between legality and legitimate was also warranted. However, he maintained that he would be leaving aside all crises and would be focusing his attention on the current problem regarding legality. During the nineteenth century, what was called a "legal state" ("Rechtsstaat") was nothing more than a "legislating state" ("Gesetzgebungsstaat") and in particular that was nothing more than a parliamentarian legislating state. This state's principle function was to generate laws and these laws were to apply universally. Thus, the legislative state was regarded as an impersonal state that generated impersonal and general laws. In such a state, there was no such thing as personal power; neither men nor authorities "dominate" ("herrschen"), only laws do so. However, even laws do not dominate; they are "*valid*" ("*gelten*") but only as norms. In such a state, there are two groups, the one group which makes the laws (the legislature) and the other group which enforces the laws. In such a state, it makes no sense to speak of orders and obedience because these laws are norms to be followed, not orders to be obeyed. This is the meaning of legality (Schmitt 1932: 7–8).

There are other political communities that vary in proximity to the legal state. The closest are the "jurisdiction states" ("Jurisdiktionstaaten") in which a judge decides which side is right in a legal conflict. The mark of such a state is the "*concrete case decision*" ("*konkrete Fall-Entscheidung*"). These states appear to be similar to the legislative states because there are norms and laws, but the difference is that there the emphasis is on a deciding judge rather than the law maker. Then, there are the "administrative states" ("Verwaltungsstaaten") in which there is the "royal personal will" ("*hoheitlichen persönlichen Willen*") and the "authoritative command" ("*authoritären Befehl*"). There are other types of states in which there is a will and commands, but they are impersonal in contrast to this type of state (Schmitt 1932: 8–9). In light of this, Schmitt insisted that the opposition which should be investigated is the opposition between legality and legitimacy and that all the other contrasts like authority and freedom can be safely ignored. In the same way, Aristotle's traditional differentiation between monarchy, oligarchy, and democracy can be set aside (Schmitt 1932: 10–11). If the parliamentarian state is composed of endless discussions and the jurisdiction state is composed of legal reasoning, the administrative state is composed of orders and obedience. As Schmitt quoted, "[t]he best in the world is a command" ("Das Beste in der Welt ist ein Befehl") (Schmitt 1932: 13). And, the legitimacy of the parliamentarian state is only its legality, whereas legitimacy is synonymous with authority. Thus, Schmitt contrasts the different natures of the state—the parliamentarian state is based upon reason in contrast to the administrative state which is founded upon the will (Schmitt 1932: 15). Schmitt had relied on Max Weber's writings in this introduction: once when Schmitt mentioned Weber's mark of a political group, once when he mentioned Weber's comments on legitimacy and legality, and once where he borrowed Weber's conception of bureaucracy as "value-free." And, finally, he employed Weber's notion of the need for the "leader-selection" ("Führerauslese") (Schmitt 1932: 11, 14, 16–17). Schmitt concluded his introduction by bemoaning that the "dynastic legitimacy of the constitutional monarchy" ("dynastische Legitimität der konstitutionellen Monarchie") has been replaced by the impersonal parliamentarian state. The past two years, Schmitt claimed, showed that the German state had been "de-weaponized and de-militarized" ("Entwaffenung und Entmilitarisierung") and that it had long ceased to exist as an "army" ("Heer"). And, he claimed that the past two years demonstrated that the German government could not guarantee "public security and order"—and he added that it could not defend it from its enemies ("öffentliche Sicherheit und Ordnung und Staatsfeindlichkeit") (Schmitt 1932: 18).

The influence of Weber is continued in the first part because Schmitt is concerned about the need for equal chances in determining political power and he noted that the term "Chance" played a prominent role in Weber's political and social-economical writings (Schmitt 1932: 30, note 1). Schmitt also noted that the Weimar constitution took a position of neutrality regarding political power, thus reinforcing the notion that the state is a neutral force and that laws are formally enforced norms. This is Kelsen's formalistic legal philosophy, but as Schmitt has argued consistently over the past decade, not only is the formal view of the state wrong in normal times, but it is extraordinarily mistaken during extraordinary conditions. Legal norms cannot provide for the "public security and order" ("öffentliche Sicherheit und Ordnung") and it cannot provide an "equal chance" ("gleiche Chance") for determining neutral laws. In other words, the legal justification for the state claiming power is no longer justifiable and a new foundation for the claim for power needs to be found (Schmitt 1932: 35, 40). Before Schmitt begins to determine that foundation, he provides a critique of the contradictions inherent in the Weimar constitution.

In the second part Schmitt argued that the Weimar constitution contained three "extraordinary legislators" ("außerordentliche Gesetzgeber"). The first is given the name "ratione materiae" and is embodied with the notion of majority rule. But Schmitt attacked it by claiming first that it was not a majority in a political sense but only in a mathematical one. That is because it can be determined by a vote of 51 to 49. In Schmitt's opinion, this is inhuman mathematics and has not much to do with democratic principles and even less with "the logic of justice, humanity, and reason" ("der Logik von Gerechtigkeit, Menschlichkeit, und Vernunft")

(Schmitt 1932: 43). Schmitt further complained that the two major divisions of the Weimar constitution were incompatible because the first section was value-free whereas the second section was value-ladened. The first section was devoted to "value free functionalism" ("wertfrei Funkionalismus") whereas the second section is focused on democratic and social values (Schmitt 1932: 52, 61). The second group of extraordinary legislators is called "ratione supremitatis." Here Schmitt indicates several instances of tension: between the value-neutral legalism of parliament and the value-filled people's principles. It is also the tension between parliament's legislating and the people's decision and the people's initiative ("Volksentscheid und Volksbegehren"). Finally, there is the tension between parliament ("ratione materiae") and the sovereign people ("ratione supremitatis") (Schmitt 1932: 62–63, 66–67). The third group of extraordinary legislators is called "ratione necessitates." Schmitt noted that this power is not explicitly spelled out in the Weimar constitution but is implicit in Paragraph 2 of Article 48. Further, this had been put into practice for the past two years. This "ratione necessitates" is in tension with the "ratione materiae" of the legislators as well as in tension with the "ratione supremitatis" of "immediately self-deciding people" ("unmittelbar selbst entscheidendes Volk") (Schmitt 1932: 71). In these three, there is the more normal power of the legislators, the less normal power of the deciding people, and finally, the abnormal power conferred by Article 48 Paragraph 2 (Schmitt 1932: 77, 79, 85). Schmitt concluded this section by noting that the practice revealed that the norms of parliament do not apply and that the idea of legal permanence is a fiction. There are only the extraordinary, but temporary, measures instituted by a "dictator" (Schmitt 1932: 87).

Schmitt concluded by observing that despite the wish to ground the Weimar constitution on legal principles and by providing three different extraordinary law givers, it only served to undermine the constitution. In the past, there may have been states with two groups of law makers, but the Weimar constitution has three and they are each extraordinary. As such, there cannot be stability in the Weimar government. Schmitt admitted that the concept of a parliamentarian state dominated state theories throughout the nineteenth century, but that its internal contradictions were not as clearly visible. The various crises that Germany had been facing during the previous decades brought those contradictions to the surface where they could not be so easily ignored. The liberal belief in pluralism and the vision that the constitution was a compromise contract were shown to be misguided and false (Schmitt 1932: 90–91). Furthermore, the pluralistic state is a "total" state, not because of strength but because of weakness. It must interfere in all aspects of life in order to survive. But its interference in economic matters undermines its liberal faith in the free market. Finally, Schmitt concluded with the claim that the Weimar government rested on a faulty legal foundation and that its constitution was really composed of two contradictory parts. What was given neutrally in the first half was undermined by the values promoted in the second. Thus, this ended the fiction of the "value and truth of the neutral majority functionalism" ("Wert und Wahrheit neutralen Mehrheitsfunktionalismus") (Schmitt 1932: 98). A new foundation for the state needs to be found—one not of empty legal formalism but one of powerful political legitimacy. That is Schmitt's concept of the political.

The choice to conclude this chapter of this book with *Der Begriff des Politischen* was a deliberate one. That is because that book is not only Schmitt's most famous and most controversial one, but it also contains much of his thinking about politics over the preceding decade. The choice to include Schmitt's book within the time frame of this book is also intentional. Although the edition from 1933 is the most famous one, because of its association with the Nazis, I cite the text from the 1932 edition which had been published by Duncker & Humblot. The move from Duncker & Humblot to the Hanseatische Verlagsanstalt in Hamburg was an indication of Schmitt's movement from scholarship to more partisanship because his new publisher was closely connected to the Nazi party.[2] An indication of this is the fact that in the 1933 edition,

[2] It is intriguing that Schmitt gives the wrong date of publication (1931) for the 1932 edition in the note that he gave at the beginning to the 1933 edition. The note reads, "Die erste Ausgabe des 'Begriffs des Politischen' erschien im August 1927 im Heidelberger Archiv für Sozialwissenschaft und Sozialpolitik; die zweite Ausgabe im Oktober 1931 bei Duncker und Humblot in München und Leipzig." ("The first edition of 'Concept of the Political' appeared in August 1927 in the Heidelberg Archive for Social Knowledge and Social Politics; the second in October 1931 by Duncker and Humblot in München and Leipzig.") It is also interesting that the Hamburg edition was printed using the old type of font (Fraktur) which was prized by the Nazis. I have found that most younger (and many older) Germans are unable to read anything printed in Fraktur. In fact,

Schmitt did not begin with a conceptual definition like he often did. He had likely learned that procedure from Max Weber. Yet, the connection with Weber still remains—because Schmitt's original article was published in Weber's journal and also because Weber's spirit is evident in *Der Begriff des Politischen.*

Instead of a definition, Schmitt began with a presupposition—that "[t]he concept of the state presupposes the concept of the political" ("Der Begriff des Staates setzt den Begriff des Politischen voraus") (Schmitt 2015: 19). He then goes on to complain that there is no clear definition either of the state or of the political. Most attempts are either negative or in opposition, and he gives the examples of "politics and economy," "politics and morality," and "politics and law." Each of these oppositions appears to be neutral and not polemical. In addition, "economy," "law," and even "morality" are used in a neutral manner which then confers a sense of neutrality to "politics." This sense of neutrality is then carried over to the state so that the state is regarded as an a-political administrative body (Schmitt 2015: 19–21). This neutrality is reinforced by the blurring of the distinction between "state" ("Staat") and "society" ("Gesellschaft") (Schmitt 2015: 23). But this neutral sense of political is not the real sense of the political.

The real political can be determined by oppositions, just as there is the opposition between "good and bad" ("Gut und Böse") in morality, the opposition between "beautiful and ugly" ("Schön und Häßlich") in aesthetics, and "useful and destructive" ("Nützlich und Schädlich") in economics. In politics, the opposition is between "friend and foe" ("Freunde und Feind") (Schmitt 2015: 25). Schmitt clarified that this opposition is not meant metaphorically or symbolically, but in its "concrete, existential sense" ("konkreter, existentieller Sinn"). He further clarifies that this opposition is not a private, psychological expression. Furthermore, "foe" ("Feind") is also neither used in the general sense nor in the private sense—it is not a sense of antipathy. It is also not a normative or a "purely mental opposition" ("'rein geistigen' Gegensätze") nor is it used in an

my local newspaper in Traunstein used to have a special section in the Saturday edition that was in Fraktur but about ten years ago, changed the type to match the rest of the paper, and kept just the title in Fraktur. Another interesting change was that normally, Schmitt's name was given as the author but in the Hanseatische edition it is given at the top of the cover as "Prof. Dr. Carl Schmitt" (Schmitt 1931, 1933).

economic sense to describe business competitors. Furthermore, the "friend-foe" opposition is not a general one nor is it used to describe a private opponent. What it is, is the opposition between "*fighting*" ("*kämpfende*") groups. A "foe" can only be a "*public* foe" ("*öffentlicher* Feind") (Schmitt 2015: 27). Schmitt drew attention to a particularity that the German language shares with many others and that is that it does not distinguish between a public use and a private one. This lack of distinction has given rise to misunderstandings, such as the frequently cited Biblical injunction to "love one's enemies." This is because this is used in a private sense and it often implies the rejection of personal hatred. In Schmitt's view, the public and political foe need not be an object of personal hatred (Schmitt 2015: 28).

Schmitt also clarifies that this struggle between "friend and foe" need not always be a struggle to death; however, he does insist that war is the greatest realization of this "doctrine of foes" ("Feindschaft"). But Schmitt downplays this aspect of the "foe" as a wartime enemy by highlighting the difference between the soldier and the politician: the former "struggles" only in exceptional instances whereas the latter spends his entire life engaged in struggling. Thus, Schmitt takes issue with Clausewitz dictum that war is the continuation of politics by other means because war is not the "goal and purpose" ("Ziel und Zweck") of politics (Schmitt 2015: 32–33). Furthermore, politics is a normal human activity and a world that did not have struggle would not be a human world. In fact, a totally peaceful world without the "friend-foe" distinction would be a world without politics (Schmitt 2015: 33, 35, 48).

Schmitt repeats his contention that the state is a political unity; thus, "sovereignty" represents this political unity. As long as there are states, there will be political unity and the claims that the state is dead are premature (Schmitt 2015: 37). Schmitt has made that claim before, just as he again criticizes Harold Laski's pluralism. Laski's doctrine is far more dangerous to the state than any workers' strikes, because Laski's pluralism undermines the political unity of the state. The state is not, as Laski believes, an association—it is not a societal manifestation like churches, clubs, and social groups. Instead, the state is a sovereign and is a unity, which is founded upon its political nature (Schmitt 2015: 38–41).

The state needs to be prepared to fight for its existence and its freedom and that means that it needs to be able to declare who its enemy is. Furthermore, its citizens must be ready to fight, which means, willing to kill and willing to risk being killed (Schmitt 2015: 42–43). And, the state needs to be ready at any time to ensure "peace, security, and order" ("Ruhe, Sicherheit, und Ordnung") (Schmitt 2015: 43). This is true regarding inner disturbances but it is more applicable regarding external foes. This means making the decision to declare who is the enemy and against whom to go to war. Returning to his notion of the willingness to die, Schmitt distinguishes between the soldier and the martyr. The soldier is willing to die to protect his state; the martyr is eager to die for the future life of his soul (Schmitt 2015: 45). There is a further difference between the soldier and the martyr and that is that the soldier adheres to the "eternal connection" ("ewige Zusammenhang") between "*protection* and *obedience*" ("*Schutz* und *Gehorsam*"). And, he draws attention to Hobbes who insisted that the single purpose of his *Leviathan* was to emphasize the necessity of "the mutual relation between Protection and Obedience" and he noted that Hobbes discovered this truth during the worse time of the civil war when all of the "legitimacy and normative illusions" ("legitimitischen und normativisitischen Illusionen") had fallen away (Schmitt 2015: 49). Not citing Hobbes, but believing that he was expressing Hobbes' view, Schmitt maintained that it is "foolish" ("Tölpelhaft") to believe that a defenseless people only has friends and that they can resist an enemy without resistance (Schmitt 2015: 50).

Again, Schmitt objected to the invocation of the pluralistic term "humanity" ("Menschheit") and he noted that "humanity" cannot wage a war because it does not have an enemy—"at least not on this planet" ("wenigstens nicht auf diesem Planeten"). Furthermore, no one can declare a war in the name of "humanity" and he repeats Proudhon's declaration that "who says humanity intends to deceive" ("Wer Menschheit sagt, will betrügen") (Schmitt 2015: 51). In fact, the whole idea of a "world state" ("Weltstaat") which would be composed of humanity would not be a political unity; hence, it would be a state only in name (Schmitt 2015: 54).

Schmitt contended that all theories of state and every political idea can be examined in an anthropological manner. And, by this he meant the issue that he had addressed earlier regarding whether human beings were "naturally good" or "naturally bad" (Schmitt 2015: 55). Many political theorists contended that humans are naturally bad. Schmitt's list included Machiavelli, Spinoza, Hobbes, and Pufendorf. That is because almost all of these thinkers believed that humans are animals and are motivated by desires and not by reason (Schmitt 2015: 55). In contrast, many liberals believed that human beings are naturally good and they emphasize their reasonableness. Hence, they regard the state as a necessary evil but insist that it should be limited in scope. The liberals often speak about the need for balance and moderation. In other words, liberals believe in neutralizing the state and depoliticizing it (Schmitt 2015: 56–57). But the liberals are optimists and they do not believe humans to be evil; hence, they reject the notion of the foe. Indeed, if one believes that good people live in peace, security, and harmony then there is no need for laws, states, or even politics. Yet, these liberals are just optimists and are not realists. In contrast, most of the major political theorists regard human nature with distrust, if not regard humans as evil by nature. Schmitt lists Machiavelli and even Fichte, but he expressly singles out Hobbes for his pessimism. Schmitt regarded Hobbes as "a great and truly systematic political thinker" ("einen großen und wahrhaft systematischen politischen Denker") who wrote about the "'Bellum' all against all" ("'Bellum' Alle gegen Alle"). But this war was not just the philosophical reflection of the competition in "society" ("Gesellschaft") that Ferdinand Tönnies discussed. Rather, it has to be regarded as the fundamental presupposition of a particular system of thought. Schmitt builds upon Hobbes' notion of war of all against all and insists that all political thinking presupposes the capacity to distinguish friend from foe (Schmitt 2015: 60–62).

Regardless of the type, liberalism believes in the individual, so it naturally rejects the notion of the state. And, liberals are optimists, so they wish to depoliticize the world. To them, the state need not exist because what is important is freedom. But this is not political freedom; this is economic freedom, hence "ethics and economy, spirit and business, education and property" ("Ethik und Wirtschaft, Geist und Geschäft, Bildung und Besitz") (Schmitt 2015: 65). For the liberal, there is no "enemy," only competition. This was derived from the Enlightenment but became more economically oriented in the nineteenth century.

Schmitt offered the following oppositions: "[F]reedom, progress and reason against feudalism, reaction, and force combined with economy, industry, and technology against state, war, and politics as parliamentarianism against dictator." As a result, war, even a successful war, is regarded as "bad business" ("schlechtes Geschäft") (Schmitt 2015: 69). For liberals, politics is to be avoided but economics pursued. And even imperialism is looked upon as an economic venture and not a political involvement (Schmitt 2015: 71).

Schmitt concluded *Der Begriff des Politischen* by recounting the steps that Europe had gone through over the previous 400 years, from theological to metaphysical, then to humanitarian-morality, and finally to economics (Schmitt 2015: 74). Accompanying these steps was the belief in reason and progress, self-mastery and education, and moral perfectionism (Schmitt 2015: 79). These steps from theological to metaphysical to moral to economics resulted in neutralizing of the spirit. What remains is merely the technical. However, Schmitt insisted that technology cannot determine domination. As he put it, "[t]he decision over freedom and servitude does not lie with technology as technology" ("Die Entscheidung über Freiheit und Knechtschaft liegt nicht in Technik als Technik"). The mood that reflected the decline of the West was not just found in Oswald Spengler's post-war book but also in the pre-war writings of Max Weber, Ernst Troeltsch, and Walther Rathenau. They all wrote about technical progress and how that was undermining the spirit of Germany and was resulting in a weakened elite. However, technology can no longer be regarded as neutral as the war had made obvious. Schmitt bemoaned the fact that the most terrifying war was conducted "in the name of peace" ("im Namen des Friedens"), the most fearful suppression was done "in the name of freedom" ("im Namen des Freiheit"), and the most terrifying inhumanity was done "in the name of humanity" ("im Namen der Menscheit"). The antithesis of mechanic and organic is unimportant; what is, is the antithesis of life and death. The first is a technical question; the second is a political one. It is the struggle of life against life that gives meaning and order to human things (Schmitt 2015: 86–87).

The writings from 1930 were legal and dry, but the writings of 1932 were full of politics and passion. Schmitt remembered his thinking and his positions from during the war and he conjoined them with his warnings about the immediate future. The polemical spirit of Max Weber can be found in these later writings. Perhaps more important, the spirit of Hobbes as the "apostle of fear" was even more present.

References

Mehring, Reinhard (2009) *Carl Schmitt. Aufstieg und Fall. Eine Biographie.* München: C.H. Beck.

Preussen (1976)[1933] *Preussen contra Reich vor dem Staatsgerichtshof. Stenogrammbericht der Verhandlungen vor dem Staatsgerichtshof in Leipzig vom 10. Bis 14. und 17. Oktober 1932. Mit einem Vorwort von Ministerialdirektor Dr. Brecht.* Glashüten im Taunus: Verlag Detlev Auvermann KG.

Schmitt, Carl (1930) "Staatsethik und pluralistischer Staat." In Schmitt 1988. 133–145.

Schmitt, Carl (1932) *Legalität und Legitimität.* München und Leipzig: Verlag von Duncker & Humblot.

Schmitt, Carl (1933) *Der Begriff des Politischen.* Hamburg: Hanseatische Verlagsanstalt Hamburg.

Schmitt, Carl (1988) *Positionen und Begriffe. Im Kampf mit Weimar-Genf-Versailles.* Berlin: Duncker & Humblot.

Schmitt, Carl (2015) *Der Begriff des Politischen. Text von 1932 mit einem Vorwort und drei Corollarien.* Berlin: Duncker & Humblot. 9., korrigierte Auflage.

Schmitt, Carl (2016)[1931] *Der Hüter der Verfassung. Anhang: Hugo Preuß. Sein Staatsbegriff und seine Stellung in der deutschen Staatslehre.* Berlin: Duncker & Humblot, Fünfte Auflage,

References

8

Schmitt and the Recovery of Law and Liberalism

Abstract This chapter contains three sections. In the first, I review Schmitt's account of fear and how he traces it back to Thomas Hobbes. In the second section, I show how Leo Strauss and Michael Oakeshott developed different and more liberal accounts of Hobbes' thinking. In the third section, I build upon Strauss and Oakeshott to offer a sketch of a defense of modern law and liberalism. During this time of Trump, Putin, Orban, and others, law and liberalism need a robust defense. Such a defense cannot be mounted here but one possible outline is sketched. Carl Schmitt may not have been a model citizen but he was a great scholar. This book is an attempt to trace his legal and political thinking between 1912 and 1932 and to show that his critiques of law and liberalism have continued relevance.

Keywords Law • Liberalism • Hobbes • Strauss • Oakeshott

Carl Schmitt was concerned about safety and security prior to the First World War, yet those issues seemed less important to him than the concept of law. However, the impact of the war and its revolutionary

© The Author(s) 2020

C. Adair-Toteff, *Carl Schmitt on Law and Liberalism*, Palgrave Studies in Classical Liberalism, https://doi.org/10.1007/978-3-030-57118-4_8

aftermath brought the concerns about safety and security to the forefront of his thinking and they remained there for the duration of the period under consideration here—meaning 1932. How much they continued to occupy Schmitt's mind past 1932 is beyond the scope of this book. By 1918 and continuing through to 1932, Schmitt was convinced that the law that he had earlier thought so highly of and the liberal thinking that he had serious concerns about, were insufficient to safeguard Germany's citizens. Hence, he spent much of this period attacking the notion of normal law and the belief in liberalism.

Schmitt was convinced that Thomas Hobbes was a kindred spirit and that Hobbes was the only genuine predecessor who recognized the need for a strong authority to lead during exceptional times. In other words, Schmitt looked to Hobbes in order to legitimize his own philosophy of political extremism. In this view, both Hobbes and Schmitt are "apostles of fear" and believe that only an individual with sufficient power can save the populace.

In this conclusion, I suggest that Schmitt misconstrued Hobbes' philosophy and I consider two thinkers who knew Schmitt's writings as well as Hobbes' work—Leo Strauss and Michael Oakeshott. In their own ways, they argue for a fuller and a richer account of Hobbes' philosophy; that is, it does much more than attempt to provide peace and security. In addition, it attempts to foster the individual's felicity within the commonwealth. In other words, Hobbes' philosophy is not just political, as Schmitt maintains, it is moral as well. Rather than seeing Hobbes as an "apostle of fear," Strauss and Oakeshott reveal him to be a defender of law and a promoter of liberalism. Granted his notion of law was less than conventional and his concept of liberalism pales against the notion of modern liberalism. But if modern liberalism has failed because of being too radical, then it is prudent to employ a type of liberalism that is more moderate, more skeptical, and, by extension, more powerful.

In what follows, I briefly revisit Schmitt's view of Hobbes and then sketch how Strauss and Oakeshott responded to Schmitt's interpretation of Hobbes. I conclude by suggesting that rather than regarding Hobbes as the "apostle of fear" that Schmitt appears to have done, that we should follow Strauss and Oakeshott in using Hobbes as a strong defender of law and of a cautious type of liberalism. Thus, Strauss and Oakeshott can serve as antidotes to the modern incarnation of the states of emergency and the alleged need for authoritarian leaders, and we can look to them as the thinkers who can help defend law and liberalism.[1]

Carl Schmitt's fullest expression of his interest in Thomas Hobbes' writings came in 1938 when he published *Der Leviathan in der Staatslehre des Thomas Hobbes.* While Schmitt was rather sympathetic to Hobbes in this work, he believed that Hobbes had ultimately failed. That is why he pointed to the "mis-hit" in his subtitle: "Sinn und Fehlschlag eines politischen Symbols" (Schmitt 1982). However, Schmitt's interest in Hobbes was generated much earlier than 1937 and this is substantiated by numerous references in *Der Leviathan* to Ferdinand Tönnies. In particular, Schmitt references the third edition of Tönnies' *Thomas Hobbes. Leben und Lehre* (Schmitt 1982: 35, note 1, 43, note 1, 44, note 1, 88, note 1, and especially 103–105). Schmitt credited Tönnies for disputing the general conception of Hobbes as a naturalistic philosopher who promoted a mechanistic view of human society. In contrast, Tönnies argued that Hobbes' philosophy was humanistic in the sense that it was fundamentally about the human will and it is this radical reevaluation of Hobbes that Schmitt approves of (Schmitt 1982: 103–105). However, Schmitt misunderstood Hobbes in many ways: first, he insisted that Hobbes was the great decisionist and he needed to be so because his concern was with "peace, security, order" ("Ruhe, Sicherheit, Ordnung") (Schmitt 1982: 82, 47, 64, 71–72, 90).[2] Second, he insisted that Hobbes failed because he did not recognize the importance of religion; Hobbes tried to make Leviathan to be like God (Schmitt 1982: 124–126). Nonetheless, Schmitt readily admitted that Hobbes was an incomparable political thinker and ranked him alongside Machiavelli and Hegel (Schmitt 1982: 129–131). Tönnies would have agreed with Schmitt's final assessment of Hobbes but would have disagreed about Hobbes being a decisionist and fully

[1] There are others who see a similarity between Strauss and Oakeshott and their interpretations of Hobbes. That does not mean that they agree with Strauss and Oakeshott. This is evident in Howard Warrender's account of Hobbes' theory of obligation (see Warrender 1957: 6–7, 142–143).

[2] It is probably not a coincidence that in the Catholic fight against the Modernists, Pope Pius X insisted that the Church was charged with maintaining order, peace, and unity. As a devote Catholic in the first decade of the twentieth century, Schmitt would have been aware of this controversy and the Pope's declaration.

preoccupied with "peace, security, and order." And, he would have bolstered his contention against Schmitt by pointing his numerous writings on Hobbes. It is important to recognize that Tönnies' reevaluation of Hobbes' philosophy prompted a number of other scholars to consider Hobbes' political philosophy in a new light, but a discussion of this is beyond the scope of this book. It is instructive to note two things: first, that the decisionist who was always concerned with "peace, security, order" was Schmitt himself; second, that Schmitt regarded Hobbes as a kindred spirit. This is evident in the short piece that Schmitt published in 1951 in commemoration of the 300th anniversary of Hobbes' Leviathan. In "Dreihundert Jahre Leviathan" Schmitt sketched a brief survey of Hobbes' role as a scapegoat in the history of political philosophy. He maintained that a scapegoat has no right to be heard and no possibility for grace. The scapegoat exists to take on the responsibility for guilt, and in Hobbes' case, it is the guilt for writing *Leviathan*, which his critics believed to be a symbol of an all-powerful state. However, the position of scapegoat was already taken by Machiavelli and Schmitt specifically mentions Michael Oakeshott's claim in the Introduction to his edition of *Leviathan* (Schmitt 1995: 152–153; Oakeshott 1975: 59). Accordingly, Oakeshott is an important voice in showing how Hobbes' political philosophy does not lead to Schmitt's, but before turning to Oakeshott, there is one other scholar who was relevant not only to Schmitt but also to Oakeshott, and that is Leo Strauss.

In numerous respects, Leo Strauss and Carl Schmitt were opposites: a Jew and a Catholic, a philosopher and a legal scholar, a fierce critic of Nazism and an arch defender of it. But both are regarded as some of the best thinkers of the twentieth century and both looked to Hobbes for a basis for their political philosophies. Moreover, it was Carl Schmitt who helped Strauss obtain a stipend which not only bolstered his academic career but probably saved his life (Smith 2009: 18–19). Strauss' preoccupation with Hobbes' philosophy began in his twenties (Strauss 2001: VIII-X). There is an entire chapter devoted to Hobbes in his *Die Religionskritik Spinozas als Grundlage seiner Bibelwissenschaft. Untersuchungen zu Spinozas Theologisch-politischen Traktat*. Written in 1928 it was published in 1930, and as the title indicates, it is focused on Spinoza's religious philosophy. The introduction seeks to locate Spinoza's theory in an historical context so Strauss examines a small number of thinkers, including Hobbes. Strauss agreed with Schmitt that Hobbes was a radical thinker; however, he disagreed with what Hobbes believed to be important. Whereas Schmitt contended that peace and security were Hobbes' main political goals, Strauss insisted that honor and satisfaction were mankind's philosophical goals (Strauss 2008: 126, 131–133). There is no doubting that Hobbes believed that the greatest evil ("malorum primum") was death and that he did not believe that there was a greatest good ("bonorum primum") but he did believe that desires and happiness were very positive things—things that the state was designed to foster (Strauss 2008: 139). In this Strauss was following Tönnies and not Schmitt (Strauss 2008: 129, note 96; 135, note 110; 138, note 121).

It is *The Political Philosophy of Hobbes* that contains Strauss' most sustained investigations into Hobbes' thinking. Written during 1934–1935 it builds on some of his unpublished writings on Hobbes, including the ideas for a book about him. But he did not publish this book in German; rather, *The Political Philosophy of Hobbes* was translated into English and was published at Oxford in 1936. Because it was published by the distinguished Clarendon Press it drew more attention than it might have otherwise. The book is not without flaws, in the Preface to the later American edition Strauss admitted that he erred in claiming that Hobbes was the founder of modern political philosophy and that that honor belonged to Machiavelli. Strauss likely got the idea from Tönnies as he was desperate to obtain a copy of his book on Hobbes (Strauss 2001: 490–491, 494). However, Strauss insisted that this distinction was a matter of degree, not of kind (Strauss 1952: viii–ix, xv).

Strauss acknowledges that Hobbes had a pessimistic view of humans but he insists that Hobbes does not view humans as intrinsically evil. The reason for this is that humans are animals and animals are neither good nor evil. While humans share natural appetites with animals, humans differ from animals because they have reason (Strauss 1952: 8–9, 14–15). It is reason which makes humans recognize that their greatest danger is to suffer a violent death at the hands of others. However, it is also reason that makes humans realize the only way to minimize this is to enter into agreements. Force is an option but not a viable one because all humans are potential enemies and one cannot struggle successfully against all

(Strauss 1952: 20–21). Thus, Strauss takes implicit issue with Schmitt's "friend/foe" distinction, an issue that he makes explicit in "Anmerkungen zu Carl Schmitt, der Begriff des Politischen." There, Strauss suggested that the "friend/foe" distinction is not only overemphasized but that it is not really clear (Strauss 2001: 220–221). Furthermore, he explicitly criticizes Schmitt for misusing Hobbes' philosophy. Whereas Hobbes began from an illiberal world to create a liberal one, Schmitt undertakes a criticism from a liberal world to create an illiberal one. Hence, Schmitt misinterprets Hobbes' liberalism for his own illiberal end (Strauss 2001: 235). Furthermore, in the book Strauss takes issue again with Schmitt: Hobbes' political philosophy is a moral one as well as a judicial one. That is because Hobbes does not think in terms of law ("virtue") but in terms of rights. That is why he does not ascribe to a natural law doctrine but one of natural right (Strauss 1952: ix). Strauss also stresses that Hobbes, like others, distinguishes between law and morality. If Schmitt dismisses morality from politics, Hobbes has it as the basis for his political philosophy (Strauss 1952: 23, 29, 108, 116, 128). This leads to another difference between Hobbes and Schmitt. Schmitt spent his life rejecting norms as being irrelevant during the "state of emergency" but Strauss insists that norms lay at the foundation of Hobbes' political philosophy. This is shown throughout Hobbes' writings (Strauss 1952: 109, 112–115). Another difference between Hobbes and Schmitt is that the former believed that the state has the duty to ensure peace at home and abroad, but it also must ensure the "freedom for individual enrichment" (Strauss 1952: 119).

Strauss concludes with some observations about Hobbes' political philosophy which directly contradict Schmitt's interpretation. First, he again emphasizes its moral basis; second, he stresses Hobbes' break with tradition; and third, political philosophy is not an art of politics but a political science (Strauss 1952: 136–137). As such, political philosophy is not concerned with persuasion and compulsion, but with arguments and reason. Strauss insists that despite Hobbes' dislike of classical philosophy, he admired Plato's philosophy. Strauss explicitly draws the connection between Hobbes and Plato and contrasts Plato's arguments with the sophistry of the Sophists. The Sophists employ rhetoric and deal with appearances; Plato utilizes arguments to discuss reality (Strauss 1952:

142–149). Plato believed in right over might and so did Hobbes. Furthermore, Hobbes was the first one to really appreciate the importance of sovereignty, but he also recognized its proper function as well as its legitimate limits. Strauss does not mention Schmitt but Schmitt's belief in power and persuasion is at odds with Strauss' belief in right and reason (Strauss 1952: 156–159). One may not follow Strauss in his ascription of classical reason to Hobbes to agree that his interpretation of Hobbes' political philosophy is a far more accurate rendering of it than that sketched by Schmitt. Furthermore, Strauss' Hobbes interpretation agrees in many respects with that of Michael Oakeshott.

That Schmitt did not mention Strauss' book on Hobbes may be due to several factors: that Schmitt did not think it necessary to mention the book or that it had appeared only in the English translation. In contrast, Michael Oakeshott not only mentioned Strauss' Hobbes book; he devoted three reviews to it. The most important one was "Dr. Leo Strauss on Hobbes" which was published in 1937 and for the most part it was a glowing review. Oakeshott maintained that part of what Strauss was doing was completely original and that part which was not was said better than anyone had prior to him (Oakeshott 1975: 141). He praised it for the power of the arguments, the clarity of style, and its moderate tone. One can contrast this with Schmitt's rhetoric, the confusing style, and his hyperbolic tone. Oakeshott noted Strauss' "admirable sense of proportion," the usefulness of the book, and his modest goal of promoting three major theses and one minor thesis. Oakeshott sets out these four as (1) that Hobbes' break with tradition, (2) that what is new is the "new moral attitude," (3) that Hobbes' life can be divided into three stages, and (4) that his contribution was to replace natural law with natural right. Oakeshott adds that Strauss correctly thinks that these four theses are linked together (Oakeshott 1975: 143–144). Strauss had taken issue with the traditional interpretation of Hobbes as one who attempted to view humans as machines. Instead, Strauss insisted that when humans moved from the state of nature to the artificial state, they became moral beings. Oakeshott observes that this moral doctrine is not only the genesis of Hobbes' theory of state but its basis (Oakeshott 1975: 146–148, 156).

In 1946 Oakeshott published an "Introduction" to Blackwell's edition of *Leviathan*. However, this was no ordinary brief introduction to the work; rather, it was an almost eighty-page commentary on it. Oakeshott believed it was the greatest if not sole masterpiece on political philosophy written in English and he attributed much of its power to the fact that it was a myth which appealed to our imaginations (Oakeshott 1975: 3, 8–9, 15). Thus far there is no real refutation of Schmitt interpretation. However, Oakeshott has many points of divergence from the picture that Schmitt had given of Hobbes' philosophy.

First, Oakeshott emphasizes the extraordinary role that reason plays in Hobbes' thinking. Humans differ from beasts in that humans have minds and that they use them to think about the past, present, and the future. In addition, reason is not absolute but conditional; that different times and places alter our knowledge (Oakeshott 1975: 7, 12, 17, 25). Second, Hobbes contrasts civil authority with natural authority. Schmitt wants us to believe that we must have a father-like authority who will know what is best for us and will demand obedience. Oakeshott contends that Hobbes believes in civil authority which is not based upon a "generational" difference but is based on mutual recognition (Oakeshott 1975: 27–29). Third, humans may be individuals and individualistic; however, they do not exist in isolation. They not only need others; they want others' praise (Oakeshott 1975: 36–38, 50). Fourth, Hobbes' philosophy has a moral component similar to the Golden Rule. Moreover, human association is wanted not just from a moral point of view but from the vantage point of mutual benefit (Oakeshott 1975: 39–40). Fifth, while "peace and security" are important components of the civil association, they are joined by the need to satisfy wants and desires. That is why it is called a "Commonwealth" (Oakeshott 1975: 42–43, 48). Sixth, Hobbes disliked religion in general and Catholicism in particular (Oakeshott 1975: 52–56). The member of the "Commonwealth" will be individualistic but will contribute to the common good. The member will be tolerant and skeptical (Oakeshott 1975: 57, 62, 64, 67). In short, he endorsed many of the tenets of liberalism. As Oakeshott observed, "[i]ndeed, Hobbes, without being himself a liberal, had in him more of the philosophy of liberalism than most of its professed defenders." Oakeshott argued that Hobbes was neither an authoritarian nor a libertine: "He perceived the folly of his age to lie in the distraction of mankind between those who claimed too much for Authority and those who claimed too much for

Liberty" (Oakeshott 1975: 67). Civil obligation is a covenant; it is a moral obligation. It is a surrender of a right (Oakeshott 1975: 72–73). What Hobbes would object to is Schmitt's own doctrine of "political theology" (see Oakeshott 1975: 76–78).

Oakeshott's clearest and most concise contrast of Hobbes' thinking with that of Schmitt occurs in "The Moral Life in the Writing of Thomas Hobbes" (1960). It is crucial to emphasize that the idea of morality is found throughout all of Oakeshott's writings on Hobbes and it serves as a contrast to Schmitt's amoral politics. Although Oakeshott intended to discuss Hobbes' type of morality in contrast to two other types, the differences with Schmitt are evident. Oakeshott claims that there are three types of morality: the communal one, the individual one, and the common good one. He has little interest in discussing the common good one and he thinks the communal one has its attractions, but his real interest is in the individual one because that is the type of morality that Hobbes has. That Hobbes stressed the individual over the community is something that Schmitt tended to downplay. It was similar to his overemphasis on Hobbes' concern about safety. And, it was typical of Schmitt to overlook the importance of voluntary contracts in Hobbes' philosophy. These are implicit criticisms in Oakeshott's "The Moral Life in the Writing of Thomas Hobbes."

Hobbes believed that humans were similar to animals in that both are moved by pleasure and pain. However, humans have memory and imagination which move people in other ways. In particular, humans seek "felicity" to seek what is best and most beneficial for them. But they also seek to avoid failure, they "dread falling behind in the race" (Oakeshott 1975: 87). As such, Hobbes insisted that humans enter into agreements of mutual trust. That is, each side believes the other will hold up their end of the bargain (Oakeshott 1975: 91, 95). This has implications for a contrast between Strauss and Oakeshott on one side and Schmitt on the other. They argue that Hobbes believed that safety was an important part of the duties of the state but that it was not the state's only duty. They also argued that Hobbes' theory of volition encompassed more than simple fear, and that pride and competition also prompted people to act. They also suggested that Hobbes was an individualist, and in particular Oakeshott believed that the individual was the basis for Hobbes' political philosophy (Tregenza 2012: 297, 304). However, that did not mean that all humans were isolated; rather, it meant that they also needed mutual trust. Finally, they suggested that trust could be gained only during normal times. Taken as a whole, the Hobbes interpretation that Strauss and Oakeshott gave undermines Schmitt's version of Hobbes' philosophy and provides an implicit rebuke of his own political theory of fear. It was Carl Schmitt who was the "apostle of fear"—not Thomas Hobbes.

Carl Schmitt was a student of Max Weber but he rejected Weber's fundamental distinction between facts and values. Weber insisted that one needed to be clear when one shifted from objective facts to subjective values. Facts may not exist in an objective world but they are subject to discussion and verification; values are necessarily subjective and therefore are not subject to scholarly dispute. This book has tried to faithfully follow Weber's fact/value distinction but now it is time to shift briefly to values.

First, Schmitt's assessment of liberalism was partially wrong. He was certainly right about the conflicts within the Weimar government but was mostly wrong about their underlying causes. It was not the Left that was causing so many disruptions but the Right. It was not liberalism per se that was malfunctioning as it was other forces that impeded its function. Second, Schmitt's assessment about laws and norms was also partially defective. He ruled them out because he believed it necessary to have a strong leader to act decisively during the "state of emergency." However, the "state of emergency" was for the most part an ideal for him and did not correspond to actual German life in the 1920s. Finally, Schmitt was wrong with the claim that only a decisive leader can save the people. Decisions need to be based upon facts and science, not on suppositions and biases. Hitler proved that to be true during the 1940s and the present corona virus pandemic proves it true now. If Schmitt's proposed solution was and is unworkable, then what is?

Again, the sketch of an answer here is subjective, but it seems that the classical liberalism that Strauss and Oakeshott saw in Hobbes is a place to start. It stressed the value of the individual but recognized that the individual was not an isolated Robinson Crusoe but was part of a state. It stressed reason but recognized that people often made choices based upon feelings. It stressed moderation, but noted that certain circumstances required more than moderation. It believed in rights as a part of law;

hence it avoided the problems inherent in natural law and legal positivism. In effect, this form of liberalism was pliant, adaptable, and reasonable. Perhaps the most important element that both Strauss and Oakeshott emphasized was that a new moral doctrine was the basis for Hobbes' political philosophy. And, perhaps what is needed is a realistic moral recovery of law and liberalism.

References

Oakeshott, Michael (1975) *Hobbes on Civil Association.* Indianapolis: Liberty Fund.

Schmitt, Carl (1982)[1938] *Der Leviathan in der Staatslehre Thomas Hobbes. Sinn und Fehlschlag eines politischen Symbols.* Stuttgart: J.C. Cotta' sche Buchhandlung.

Schmitt, Carl (1995) "Dreihundert Jahre Leviathan. Zum 5. April 1951." In Schmitt, Carl *Staat, Grossraum, Nomos: Arbeiten aus dem Jahren 1916–1969.* Berlin: Duncker & Humblot.

Smith, Steven B., editor (2009) *The Cambridge Companion to Leo Strauss.* Cambridge: Cambridge University Press.

Strauss, Leo (1952)[1936] *The Political Philosophy of Hobbes. Its Basis and Its Genesis.* Translated by Elsa M. Sinclair. Chicago: University of Chicago Press.

Strauss, Leo (2001) *Hobbes' politische Wissenschaft und zugehörige Schriften-Briefe.* Herausgegeben von Heinrich und Wiebke Meier. Stuttgart/Weimar: Verlag J.B. Metzler. *Gesammelte Schriften* 3.

Strauss, Leo (2008) *Die Religionskritik Spinozas und zugehörige Schriften.* Stuttgart/Weimar: Verlag J.B. Metzler. *Gesammelte Schriften* 1. Dritte Auflage.

Tregenza, Ian (2012) "Oakeshott's contribution to Hobbes scholarship." In Podoksik 2012. 298–318.

Warrender, Howard (1957) *The Political Philosophy of Hobbes. His Theory of Obligation.* Oxford: At the Clarendon Press.

Index[1]

A
Abdication, 2, 9
Absolutism, 28, 56–58
Abstraction, 14, 85
Accomplishment, 10
Activities, 9, 87, 88, 107
Allegiance, 2, 93
Americans, 3, 18, 42, 81, 117
Anschütz, Gerhard, 40, 76, 98, 99
Antidote, 62, 115
"Apostle of Fear"
"Das Ausführungsgesetz zu Art. 48 der Reichsverfassung (sog. Diktaturgesetz)," 54
"Das Reichsgericht als Hüter der Verfassung," 76, 94
"Der Begriff der modernen Demokratie in seinem Verhältnis zum Staatsbegriff.," 49
"Der Begriff des Politischen.," 6, 48, 65, 66, 101, 105, 106, 110, 118
"Der Gegensatz von Parlamentarismus und moderner Massendemokratie," 62
"Der Reichsgericht als Hüter der Verfassung," 87
"Zu Friedrich Meineckes 'Idee der Staatsräson,'" 59
Aristotle, 80, 102
Article, 2, 18, 36, 48, 65, 75, 92

[1] Note: Page numbers followed by 'n' refer to notes.

© The Author(s) 2020

C. Adair-Toteff, *Carl Schmitt on Law and Liberalism*, Palgrave Studies in Classical Liberalism, https://doi.org/10.1007/978-3-030-57118-4

Article 48, 5, 36, 37, 50–54, 96, 98, 100
Athens, 64
Australia, 64
Authority, 27, 28, 33, 35, 37–39, 41, 43–45, 48, 50, 52, 55, 56, 58, 59, 68, 70, 79, 86, 99, 101, 102, 114, 120

B

Ballot, 71, 72, 81
Baudelaire, Charles, 27
Beasts, 34, 120
Bentham, Jeremy, 63, 81
Bismarck, Otto von, 45, 58, 66
Bodin, Jean, 35, 39, 40, 57
Bonn, 48, 75
Boss, 81
Britain, 2
Brothers Grimm, 71
Budget, 70

C

Calker, Fritz von, 11
Case, 11, 14, 18, 19, 22, 39, 56, 64, 77, 82, 87, 90, 97–100, 97n1, 116
Cassandra, 48
Chaos, 2, 23, 26, 33, 35, 38, 40, 47–59, 78, 91–111
Chicken, 14
Christ, Jesus, 17, 45
Church, 14, 27, 28, 32, 35, 38, 45, 57, 58, 66, 67, 93, 107, 115n2
Circumstances, 2, 4, 19, 23, 35, 53, 78, 97, 100, 122
Citizen, 6, 23, 33, 36, 38, 52, 64, 67–69, 81, 82, 84, 85, 89, 93, 95, 98, 108, 114
Civil authorities, 19, 120
Civil courts, 19
Clode, Charles M., 22
Cohen, Hermann, 13–15, 13n12
Community, 27, 28, 30, 65, 67, 72, 95, 102, 121
Competition, 43, 95, 109, 121
Concern, 2, 5, 6, 13, 22, 30, 32, 33, 40, 41, 45, 51–53, 71, 77, 81, 99, 114, 115, 121
Constitution, 2, 35, 48, 61, 77, 93
Contract, 17, 30, 43, 64, 78, 79, 87, 88, 94, 105, 121
Convictions, 4, 19, 41, 57, 58, 63, 64, 78, 86, 89
Copernicus, 29
Corruption, 62, 70
Cortés, Donoso, 41
Critic, 1, 116
Cromwell, Oliver, 35
Crown jurist, 2, 92

D

Danger, 3, 4, 22, 51, 87, 89, 96, 99, 117
Declaration, 22, 28, 49, 88, 108, 115n2
Decrees, 41, 57
Defeat, 2, 5, 25
Defense, 1, 4, 6, 7, 22, 49, 58, 99
Democracy
  Der Begriff des Politischen, 6
  Der Führer schütz das Recht, 2
  Der Hüter der Verfassung, 88, 94

Der Leviathan in der Staatslehre Thomas Hobbes. Sinn und Fehlschlag eines politischen Symbol, 115
Der Wert des Staates und die Bedeutung des Einzelnen, 13
Descartes, Rene, 16, 29
Despair, 10
Despots, 57, 81
Deutsche Gesellschaft für Soziologie, 14n12
Dictatorial powers
Die Diktatur. Vom den Anfängen des modernen Souveränitätsgedanken bis zum proletarischen Klassenkampf, 33
Die geistesgeschichtliche Lage des heutigen Parlamentarismus, 41, 49
Dictatorship
"Die Diktatur des Reichspräsidenten nach Artikel 48 der Weimarer Verfassung," 50
"Die Einwirkungen des Kriegszustandes auf das ordentliche strafprozessuale Verfahren," 19
"Diktatur," 21
"Diktatur und Belagerungszustand," 21
"Dreihundert Jahre Leviathan," 116
Discussion, 2, 3, 5, 6, 11n3, 11n4, 21, 34, 35, 38, 43, 58, 62, 63, 82, 83, 94, 99, 102, 116, 122
Disenchantment, 10
Disorder, 5, 35, 48, 51, 68
Dorotić, Pawla, 10
Dostoevsky, Fyodor, 45

E

Ebert, Friedrich, 55, 83, 97
Economics, 2, 5, 19, 25, 43, 45, 46, 63, 64, 66, 67, 75, 76, 84, 89, 94, 95, 105–107, 109, 110
Education, 30, 58, 83, 109, 110
Egg, 14
Emergencies, 3, 10, 20, 21, 34–36, 38–40, 51, 53–55, 96, 115, 118, 122
Enlightenment, 21, 26, 27, 37, 38, 41, 43, 81, 109
Equality, 3, 6, 49, 64, 80, 81, 83, 86
Europe, 4, 18, 32, 70, 83, 110
Exception, 4, 11n2, 39, 40

F

Facts, 4, 11n4, 14, 15, 20, 21, 32, 43, 44, 50–52, 56, 58, 62–64, 66, 69, 70, 78, 81, 88, 98, 105, 105n2, 107, 108, 110, 122
Faith, 23, 44, 45, 105
Federalism, 94, 95
Fichte, Johannes Gottlob, 27–29, 109
Fiction, 12, 50, 104, 105
First World War, 18, 23, 52, 78, 113
Fool, 20
Foundation, 2, 15n13, 44, 58, 62, 73, 85, 93, 103, 105
France, 2, 42, 64

French Revolution, 21, 27, 28, 32–36, 42, 45, 58, 86, 96
Friedrich the Great, 56, 57
Future, 2, 26, 33, 44, 48, 49, 59, 66, 70, 85, 108, 111, 120

G
Germany, 1–5, 9, 10, 18, 25, 27, 33, 36, 47, 48, 51, 55, 58, 59, 61, 70, 75, 76, 84–86, 91, 95, 97, 100, 104, 110, 114
Gesestz und Urteil, 10
Goethe, Johannes von, 27, 28
Government, 5, 37, 45, 47, 52, 58, 63, 66, 70, 71, 73, 82, 85, 89, 91, 93, 95, 97–101, 103–105, 122
Grand Inquisitors, 38, 45
Greeks, 64, 80
Grotius, Hugo, 68

H
Harmony, 43, 109
Hatred, 18, 45, 73, 107
Hegel, Georg Wlhelm Friedrich, 15, 29, 32, 41, 58, 92, 93, 115
Heraclitus, 4
Hindenburg, Paul von, 97, 101
History, 2, 5, 15, 26, 29–35, 37, 40, 42, 56, 58, 64, 80, 86, 90, 94, 98, 100, 116
Hobbes, Thomas, 3, 33, 48, 68, 92, 114
"Hugo Preuß. Sein Staatsbegriff und seine Stellung in der Deutschen Staatslehre," 63, 85
Humanity, 31, 44, 45, 69, 93, 103, 108, 110
Human rights, 22, 27
Humboldt, Wilhelm von, 27

I
Identity, 42, 50, 79, 81, 82
Impartiality, 95, 96
Inequality, 49, 81, 86
Inflation, 5, 25, 45, 47, 59, 61, 75, 84
Initiative, 70, 71, 73, 104
Institution, 16, 28, 32, 42, 57, 62, 95
Instrument, 17, 35, 36, 82, 89
Insurrection, 19
Intellectuals, 18, 93
Interpretation, 6, 51, 52, 70, 84, 100, 114, 115n1, 118–120, 122
Investigation, 11, 19, 92, 117

J
Jaffé, Edgar, 55
Jellinek, Georg, 38, 100

K
Kant, Immanuel, 15–17, 29, 32, 40, 92, 93
Kantorowicz, Hermann, 11n4, 13, 13–14n12
Kapp Putsch, 25
Kelsen, Hans, 15, 38, 40, 41, 76, 88, 103

L

Laski, Harold, 66, 69, 93, 107
Law, 1, 10, 26, 48, 62, 76, 93, 113
Lederer, Emil, 67
Legalität und Legitimität, 6, 101
Legal concept
"Recht und Macht," 13, 14, 20, 21
"Reichspräsident und Weimarer Verfassung," 55
"Soziologie des Souveränitätsbegriffes und politische Theologie," 37
"Staatsethik und pluralistischer Staat," 92, 94
Legitimacy, 6, 41, 79, 102, 105, 108
Lessing, Gottfried, 27
Liberalism, 1–7, 10, 13, 16, 23, 26, 38, 41–43, 48, 58, 62–66, 69, 72, 79, 81–83, 85, 86, 97, 109, 113–123
Life, 3, 5, 7, 9, 10, 25, 32, 37, 44, 47, 48, 52, 67, 76, 77, 91, 92, 105, 107, 108, 110, 116, 118, 119, 122
Luther, Martin, 34

M

Machiavelli, Niccolo, 34, 57, 79, 109, 115–117
Marburg School, 15
Master, 1, 17
Measures, 1, 3, 10, 19, 23, 36, 53, 54, 62, 96, 98–100, 104
Mechanism, 16, 44, 57
Mehring, Reinhard, 7, 11n2, 92
Meierhenrich, Jens, 6, 11n2
Meinecke, Friedrich, 56, 57
Mill, John Stuart, 97
Minnesota, 18
Mommsen, Theodor, 71
Monarch, 35, 42, 53, 56, 57, 79
Monarchy, 27, 35, 42, 50, 63, 77, 82, 95, 102, 103
Morality, 15, 56, 57, 106, 118, 121
Müller, Adam, 28
Murder, 19
Mystic, 30

N

Nature, 26, 29–31, 33, 34, 44, 45, 58, 69, 71, 78, 90, 92, 99, 102, 107, 109, 119
Naumann, Friedrich, 63
Nazis, 1, 3, 98, 100, 105, 105n2
Neutrality, 89, 95–97, 103, 106
New York, 76
Nietzsche, Friedrich, 27, 30, 92
Norm, 14, 16, 20, 38, 68, 77–79, 87, 88, 93, 94, 96, 101–104, 118, 122
Novalis, 27, 32

O

Oakeshott, Michael, 6, 114, 115n1, 116, 119–123
Order, 2, 11n4, 26, 48, 67, 77, 94, 114
Outsider, 85, 92
Owner, 66, 67, 83

P

Pamphlet, 85, 87, 101
Papen, Franz von, 97
Parliament, 5, 42, 43, 45, 53, 55–57, 62–64, 77, 83, 95, 97, 100, 104
Partisanship, 4, 105
Philosophy, 1–7, 14, 15, 21, 29–33, 41, 58, 68, 92, 93, 103, 114–123
Plato, 16, 93, 118, 119
Plettenberg, 3
Politische Romantik, 26, 27, 32, 33
Pope, 17, 45, 115n2
Popitz, Johannes, 76, 88–90, 95
Positionen und Begriffe. In Kampf mit Weimar-Genf-Versailles 1923–1939, 4
Prague, 76
Press, 18, 37, 43, 51, 54, 81
Presuppositions, 63, 106, 109
Preuss, Hugo, 2, 84–86
Principle, 42, 43, 64, 71, 72, 77, 79, 81–83, 89, 101, 103, 104
Propagandists, 3
Protector, 3, 87–89, 94
Psychology, 11n3
Public opinion, 43, 64, 79, 81

R

Rabble, 34
Rathenau, Walther, 25, 110
Reason, 12, 20, 26, 27, 29, 37, 43–45, 57, 68, 83, 92, 98, 102, 103, 109, 110, 117–120, 122
Recovery, 113–123
Referendum, 70, 73, 82, 84
Regime, 3, 28
Regular courts, 19, 52
Respect, 5, 14, 17, 44, 48, 70, 73, 78, 79, 82, 85, 116, 119
Revolution, 2, 9, 21, 23, 27–29, 32, 41, 57
Romantics, 26–33, 57
Römischer Katholizismus und politische Form, 44
Rousseau, Jean-Jacques, 27,28, 37, 42, 57, 64, 72, 73, 80
Russian Revolution, 33
Russians, 3

S

Safety, 23, 36, 59, 69, 98, 113, 114, 121
Schlegel, Friedrich, 27, 28, 32
Schleiermacher, Friedrich, 32
Scholarship, 4, 7, 58, 105
Science, 15, 58, 85, 118, 122
Sea, 17, 17–18n16
Service, 10, 45
Simons, Oliver, 6, 11n2
Slave, 17, 64
Society, 15, 27, 44, 65, 67, 93–95, 106, 109, 115
Sociology, 11, 11n3, 37
Sohm, Rudolph, 44
Soldiers, 56, 107, 108
Sombart, Werner, 55
Sophists, 118
Spinoza, Barach, 29, 109, 116
Staat, Großraum, Nomos. Arbeiten aus den Jahren 1916–1969, 60
Stammler, Rudolf, 11n4, 13–15, 13n12

State, 2, 10, 26, 49, 64, 76, 92, 115
State of exception, 34, 40
State of siege, 21, 22, 36
Strassburg, 10
Strauss, David Friedrich, 32
Study, 21, 30
System, 29, 43, 77, 82, 83, 95, 101, 109

T

Talk, 3, 50, 82
Test lecture, 19
Thinkers, 1, 5, 13n12, 27, 28, 34, 37, 38, 41, 43, 56, 57, 66, 67, 80, 86, 92, 93, 97, 109, 114–117
Third Reich, 2, 3
Thoma, Richard, 49–50, 56
Tolerance, 3, 13, 27, 92
Tönnies, Ferdinand, 27, 65, 109, 115–117
Tradition, 26–28, 38, 45, 65, 118, 119
Tranquility, 36, 51
Tribunals, 19, 51, 52, 63
True will, 12, 50
Turkey, 64
Tyranny, 57

U

Union, 22, 30, 66, 67, 93, 95
Unity, 2, 35, 65–67, 69, 73, 77–80, 82, 84, 88, 89, 93, 94, 97, 107, 108, 115n2
Universality, 17
Unrest, 2, 5, 9, 21, 22, 59, 98

V

Vaihinger, Hans, 92
Value judgments, 4, 49
Values, 4, 5, 12, 13, 16, 33, 62, 93, 104, 105, 122
  Verfassungsrechtliche Aufsätze aus den Jahren 1924–1954, 75
Victory, 2, 9, 42
  Volksentscheid und Volksbegehren. Ein Beitrag zur Auslegung der Weimarer Verfassung und Zur Lehre von unmittelbaren Demokratie, 70

W

War, 2, 3, 9, 18, 19, 21–23, 33, 34, 36, 40, 45, 52, 59, 66–69, 80, 99–101, 107–110, 113
Weber, Max, 4, 13–14n12, 37, 44, 49, 55, 63, 73, 86, 102, 103, 106, 110, 111, 122
Weimar, 2, 36, 47, 61, 75, 91, 122
Will of god, 20
Will of the law, 11, 12
Will of the law giver, 11
Will of the people
  "Zehn Jahre Reichsverfassung," 84
Will to power, 30
Witness, 88
Wittmeyer, Leo, 76
Women, 42
World, 16, 18, 20, 21, 29, 41, 61, 64, 69, 75, 85, 91, 102, 107, 109, 118, 122
World state, 69, 108

Z

Zeppelin airships, 18

The manufacturer's authorised representative in the EU is Springer Nature Customer Service Centre GmbH, Europaplatz 3, 69115 Heidelberg, Germany. If you have any concerns regarding our products, please contact ProductSafety@springernature.com

Printed and bound by CPI Group (UK) Ltd, Croydon, CR0 4YY
28/09/2026
02224083-0007